GERARD MANLEY HOPKINS

Priest and Poet

JOHN PICK

SECOND EDITION

GREENWOOD PRESS, PUBLISHERS
WESTPORT, CONNECTICUT

Library of Congress Cataloging in Publication Data

Pick, John, 1911-
  Gerard Manley Hopkins, priest and poet.

  Reprint of the ed. published by Oxford
University Press, New York, which was issued as
GB171 in series: A Galaxy book.
  Bibliography: p.
  Includes index.
  1. Hopkins, Gerard Manley, 1844-1889.
2. Poets, England--19th century--Biography.
3. Jesuits--Great Britain--Biography. I. Title.
PR4803.H44Z77 1978   821'.8   78-14838
ISBN 0-313-20589-2

This reprint has been authorized by the Oxford University Press.

Reprinted in 1978 by Greenwood Press, Inc.
51 Riverside Avenue, Westport, CT. 06880

Printed in the United States of America

10 9 8 7 6 5 4 3 2 1

Contents

Chapter		Page
I.	The Star of Balliol	1
II.	Ad Majorem Dei Gloriam	24
III.	The Wreck of the Deutschland	40
IV.	Poems, 1877–8	52
V.	Priest and Preacher, 1877–81	73
VI.	Poems, Tertianship, More Poems	87
VII.	Dublin and Desolation	106
VIII.	Last Poems, 1884–9	138
	Appendix	157
	References	160
	Index	167

ERRATA

On page 85, line 17, *news* should be *views*.

On page 156, line 20, *specific* should be *generic*.

Foreword

THE distinction of this book by Dr. Pick is that it treats of Gerard Hopkins as priest and poet. I do not say priest as well as poet, for Dr. Pick shows most convincingly that the two titles are inseparable in Hopkins.

Many articles and reviews have appeared which without collusion agree in this: that the long dead Jesuit poet, ignored in his lifetime and not resuscitated till 1918, must be ranked as amongst the first English-speaking poets of the nineteenth century, and perhaps of any century. These writers have dealt with him as a poet, but for the most part they have been chary of discussing the priest. Some have hinted that he was a poet despite his priesthood. They feel that his religious vocation throttled him—all religion and particularly the Catholic religion being to them "allergic" to poetry and love of natural things and persons, or because Jesuit discipline and spirituality frown on verse-making as a useless occupation. The result has been that so far no one has penetrated to his secret, which explains both the character and the power of this single-eyed poet. The secret lies in the unity of poet, priest, and Jesuit, in Hopkins; and this marks off Dr. Pick's book from all others. Knowing what the Catholic Faith means and having studied with rare insight and appreciation the form of spirituality which distinguishes the Jesuit, he is able to show convincingly that Hopkins' poetry is a loving regard of God and His creatures in the light of the Exercises of St. Ignatius and the sacramental doctrine of the Church.

Once this is grasped the poems fall into order and take on meaningfulness. We see the change-over in maturity: the preoccupation with the true "scape" of things designed by God, the sense of the passing loveliness of earthly things and the need of dedicating them through the Cross to Christ. Perhaps, as so many Victorian spiritual writers did, he tended to over-emphasize the danger of mortal beauty and the proximity of sin, but who are we in these days, when evil wills twist the souls of youth and demolish ancient beauties, to criticize him?

I am so glad that Dr. Pick dismisses the superficial talk of mystic "dark nights" when discussing the sombre sonnets of Hopkins' last years. They obviously fall into what is well known as the season of dry and dark faith, a season during which most good people are deprived of all the old sensible delights they

vii

formerly enjoyed when thinking of God and all His saints. Faith is left without its natural supports and never wavers—and so prepares the way for a fuller dependence on God in hope and a greater union in Charity.

Writing as I do from a land noisy and made horrible by modern war, I am comforted to find a true English poet so richly honoured; and it is in the silence which is eloquent of Hopkins and in his power to see in "Wrecks" and "Heraclitean Fire" a "lovely-felicitous Providence" that one relives the Truth which comes from God, when lies and evil philosophies, bursting with bombs into our lives, try to hide it.

M. C. D'ARCY, S.J.

Campion Hall, Oxford: 2nd July, 1941.

Acknowledgements

I AM deeply indebted to the Rev. Martin C. D'Arcy, S.J., for his permission to examine the unpublished Hopkins manuscripts at Campion Hall and for his kindly encouragement and his gracious foreword; to Miss Helen C. White for her sympathetic direction and valuable suggestions; to Rev. John Louis Bonn, S.J., and Rev. Joseph Husslein, S.J., for their helpful criticisms; and to Mr. Francis J. O'Malley, Sister Berchmans Louise, S.N.D., Mr. William Casey, S.J., and Mr. Thomas Grace, S.J., and many friends for their generous aid.

For permission to make quotations from copyright material I am obliged to Geoffrey Bles Ltd. and to Charles Scribner's Sons for Maritain's *True Humanism*; to Kegan Paul, Trench, Trubner and Co. Ltd. for Poulain's *Graces of Interior Prayer*; to Chatto and Windus Ltd. for Leavis' *New Bearings in English Poetry*; to the executrix, to Messrs. Hodder and Stoughton, and to Doubleday Doran Co. for Chesterton's *St. Francis of Assisi*; to Martin Secker & Warburg Ltd. and Alfred A. Knopf for Machen's *Hieroglyphics*; to P. J. Kenedy and Sons for Mullan's translation— and to A. R. Mowbray & Co. for Longridge's translation—of the *Spiritual Exercises of St. Ignatius*; to Burns, Oates, and Washbourne Ltd. for Thompson's translation of *Letters and Writings of Marie Lataste*; to Longmans Green and Company Ltd. for Liddon's *Life of Edward B. Pusey*, Ward's *Life of John Henry Cardinal Newman* and Newman's *Loss and Gain*; to the Macmillan Company for Pater's *Renaissance*, and to Nicholson & Watson and the Macmillan Company for quotations from Father D'Arcy's essay in *Great Catholics*.

To the editors of *The Month* I am grateful for their permission to make use of articles which I published in that magazine.

And my debt is great to the Oxford University Press and especially to Mr. Gerard Hopkins who made possible the publication of this book, and to Mr. Vincent Turner, S.J., of Campion Hall, who made corrections in it.

Foreword to second edition

IN the midst of the fluctuations of contemporary taste, Hopkins is established more securely than ever. One hundred years ago, in 1866, he was an Oxford undergraduate. Today he appears in almost every important collection of poetry, and, indeed, he is the only nineteenth-century poet who is included in the anthologies of both the Victorians and the moderns, for now both are almost equally eager to claim him.

Although he died unacclaimed at the age of forty-five in 1889, his poetry was not published until 1918—almost thirty years after his death. Prophetically during his lifetime Hopkins had written of his poetry to his lifelong friend and correspondent, Robert Bridges: "If you do not like it, it is because there is something you have not seen and I see . . . and if the whole world agreed to condemn it or see nothing in it I should only tell them to take a generation and come to me again."

Since Bridges' first edition of the poetry of Hopkins in 1918 the evaluation of Hopkins has gone through great changes:

What Bridges—"like a great dragon folded in the gate to forbid all entrance"—in his oft-quoted "Preface to Notes" considered defects of Hopkins, "faults of taste . . . rude shocks of his purely artistic wantonness . . . which a reader must have courage to face," —these are now considered his virtues.

Reaction to Hopkins in the 1920s was either violent rejection or enthusiastic but often uncritical acclaim. Thus, comments ranged all the way from "Any reader is to be forgiven who feels life is too short to work through torment to an understanding of his prosody" to "As a metrist he had no equal in English"; or from "I cannot believe that these poems deserve or will receive attention from even the most determined seeker after novelties" to "When the history of the 1920s comes to be written by a dispassionate critic, no influence will rank in importance with that of Gerard Manley Hopkins."

Most early critics saw Hopkins as a maverick, born out of his due time, an idiosyncratic poet without affinities. Only recently have critics seen his poetry as a synthesis of the new and the old, the revolutionary and the traditional.

In recent decades what is in America called the "new criticism", has meticulously explored the text and texture of his poems, finding them ever richer and more multi-dimensional so that one critic brought to a close a two-volume study of the poet with, "After an intensive reading of Hopkins, most other English poetry seems outwardly facile and in varying degrees inadequate."

Further indication of a shift in the evaluation of Hopkins is that prior to the appearance of the present book, *Gerard Manley Hopkins: Priest and Poet*, there was a tendency to consider that the priest in Hopkins stifled—or even killed—the poet. "His religious vocation," contended C. Day Lewis in 1934, "puts a wall between his life and ours only reminiscent of the wall of a madhouse."

Now instead, it is recognized that his poetry was either the result of the organic and integral collaboration of the priest and the poet, of sensibility and of belief, or, on the other hand, that it was an inscape of the tension between the two, a triumphant and victorious expression of his inner drama, "the war within", as he refers to it in one of his most powerful sonnets.

One of Hopkins' friends, R. W. Dixon, attempted to characterize this as "something I cannot describe, but known to myself by the inadequate word *terrible pathos*—something of what you call temper in poetry: a right temper which goes to the point of the terrible: the terrible crystal."

It is true that the poet's religious dedication probably restricted the quantity of his poems but they correspondingly gained in intensity and in those very qualities which every critic now considers as constituting the greatness of Hopkins.

Since the first appearance of this introductory biographical-critical book a vast amount of criticism has appeared, and more primary materials have become available. *Further Letters of Gerard Manley Hopkins* has been expanded by Claude Colleer Abbott to include important family correspondence, *The Journals and Papers of Gerard Manley Hopkins* edited by Humphry House and completed by Graham Storey has replaced *The Note-Books and Papers of Gerard Manley Hopkins*, and *Sermons and Devotional Writings of Gerard Manley Hopkins* has been edited by Christopher Devlin.

Nevertheless, the general thesis of *Gerard Manley Hopkins: Priest and Poet* needs little alteration in its essentials. The changes and corrections are therefore minor in the present edition.

Some evidence will always be missing, particularly because of lost manuscripts and the destruction by Bridges of his own letters, and there is still no definitive life of Hopkins.

January 1966   JOHN PICK
Marquette University,
Milwaukee, Wisconsin, U.S.A.

GERARD MANLEY HOPKINS

The Star of Balliol

IN his prefatory sonnet to the 1918 edition of the poems of
Gerard Manley Hopkins, Robert Bridges wrote,

Yet love of Christ will win man's love at last.

But while interest in Hopkins the technician has been dis-
proportionately great, so many have been the misconceptions and
misunderstandings of his spiritual life that a study of his religious
thought and development, the very inspiration and substance of
his poetry as of his life, is essential to an understanding of this
poet who was a priest as well.

In spite of the fact that most of the available correspondence
of the poet, and most of his significant note-books, diaries, and
papers have now been published, nevertheless the student of
Hopkins is at every hand circumscribed by the limitations of his
materials. There are, for instance, no family letters, while one of
the greatest losses has been the disappearance or destruction of
what must have been the most revelatory of his writings, his
spiritual diary. But such materials as do survive provide the
general outlines of the development of one of the most extraordin-
ary of Victorians.

There is really only one date in the life of Gerard Manley
Hopkins that has any great significance. It is the great dividing
point of his life. On one side is the unformed youth, on the other
is the Jesuit priest. On the one side is his early verse, on the
other is his great poetry. In September, 1868, when Hopkins at
the age of twenty-four entered the Jesuit novitiate, the entire
direction of his life was changed.

But this decision to turn upon the years of his youth was preceded by an heroic struggle to find a solution for the problems
which confronted him.

"The child is father to the man."
How can he be? The words are wild,

wrote Gerard Manley Hopkins in one of those sets of comic
verses with which he delighted to annoy and to amuse his friends.
But in his case both the poet and the priest of later years are

germinally present in the young Gerard, whose native temperament and character showed themselves early in his boyhood.

To begin with, he was so fortunate as to be born into a family which encouraged his precocious and artistically sensitive disposition. His was a family in which no ordinary son would be expected, for his father had himself published a volume of poems; uncles on both sides of his family were painters; his brothers, Arthur and Everard, were to become artists; one sister did facile sketches, another wrote competent verses, and still another was to help him all his life with his music.

Before Gerard entered Highgate School in 1854 he had been tutored at home in music and drawing by a gifted aunt. When he went to southern Germany with his father in 1860, he sent home sketches of Bavarian peasants, and at school he filled note-books with drawings, finished and in minute detail, of landscapes, trees, flowers, cloud-effects, and other manifestations of natural beauty.

Even more of an index to the sensibility of the boy in his teens are the verses he wrote when he was at Highgate, where he distinguished himself as a scholar and poet.

The most remarkable of Hopkins' school poems, "A Vision of the Mermaids", is also the most characteristic of his early work, for in it his native sensitivity and exuberant delight in sensuous beauty find their most concentrated expression. Little more than a collection of sensuous images strung together on a very tenuous theme, this "little" is much, for it suggests the influence of Keats as well as Spenser. The impassioned sensuous apprehension of the world about him pulses in every one of the one hundred and forty-three lines; the excited couplets are loaded and packed with sharp sense-perception, "by hot pantings blown":

> Plum-purple was the west; but spikes of light
> Spear'd open lustrous gashes, crimson-white;
> .   .   .   .
> Fair beds they seem'd of water-lily flakes
> Clustering entrancingly in beryl lakes:
> Anon, across their swimming splendour strook,
> An intense line of throbbing blood-light shook
> A quivering pennon; then, for eye too keen,
> Ebb'd back beneath its snowy lids, unseen.
> Now all things rosy turn'd: the west had grown
> To an orb'd rose, which, by hot pantings blown
> Apart, betwixt ten thousand petall'd lips

By interchange gasp'd splendour and eclipse.
The zenith melted to a rose of air;
The waves were rose-lipp'd; the crimson glare
Shower'd the cliffs and every fret and spire
With garnet wreaths and blooms of rosy-budded fire.

In the above he appeals primarily to the eye, but he could invoke the senses of taste, touch, and smell, in compressed lines:

Soon—as when Summer of his sister Spring
Crushes and tears the rare enjewelling,
And boasting "I have fairer things than these"
Plashes amidst the billowy apple-trees
His lusty hands, in gusts of scented wind
Swirling out bloom till all the air is blind
With rosy foam and pelting blossom and mists
Of driving vermeil-rain; and, as he lists,
The dainty onyx-coronals deflowers,
A glorious wanton.

But perhaps the quality of Hopkins' school verse is best epitomized by a couplet of another Highgate poem:

—A little sickness in the air
From too much fragrance everywhere.

Of no one does the early Hopkins remind the reader so much as of the young Keats. Later in his life Hopkins, in possession of an aesthetic which he developed during his years in the Jesuit novitiate, wrote a criticism of Keats in which it is possible that he was drawing his own portrait and evaluating his own youthful work. Coventry Patmore, his friend of later years, had written a review of Colvin's life of Keats; Hopkins read the review and, while disagreeing with Patmore's more severe strictures on Keats' "luxuriating", wrote:

It is impossible not to feel with weariness how his verse is at every turn abandoning itself to an unmanly and enervating luxury. It appears too that he said something like "O, for a life of impressions instead of thoughts!" . . . he lived in mythology and fairyland the life of a dreamer.

On the other hand, he pays tribute to latent powers of another kind:

Nevertheless, I feel and see in him the beginnings of something opposite to this, of an interest in higher things, and of powerful and active thought. . . . His mind had, as it seems to me, the distinctly masculine powers in abundance, his character the manly virtues, but while he gave himself up to dreaming and self-indulgence, of course, they were in abeyance. Nor do I mean that he would have turned to a life of virtue—only God can know that—, but that his genius would have taken to an austerer utterance in art. Reason, thought, what he did not want to live by, would have asserted itself presently and perhaps have been as much more powerful than that of his contemporaries as his sensibility or impressionableness, by which he did want to live, was keener and richer than theirs.[1]

Hopkins recognized the weakness of the youthful Keats, but did he recognize his own weakness as a youth? While we have seen that in the pursuit of beauty, sensuous apprehension was almost a part of Hopkins' native temperament, we have yet to see anything in him that would allow us to say, "The child is father to the man", in relation to his later attempts to control his experience of beauty and to direct that experience as an act of religious worship.

Such a "list or leaning" was, however, almost as inherent as his capacity for artistic sensibility, though it was for the most part "in abeyance", certainly not yet brought into relationship to his art. Already, nevertheless, he was determined to gain self-mastery.

Stories survive from his Highgate days of heroic efforts at abstinence. For instance, once he went for a week without drinking any liquids. There is always a danger in reading biography backwards and seeing too clearly in the distance the acorn which was later to become the oak. There is such a danger here: no evidence will support us if we say that such deeds of the youthful Hopkins were acts of religious renunciation in an effort to discipline the senses, but we are justified in saying that these acts of self-denial are indications of an early determination to master himself, of a courageous strength of will. And we know that as soon as he got to Oxford the same two strains so far revealed, the aesthetic and the ascetic, were to comprise his most important preoccupations.

Such then was the temperament and "bent of being" in the nineteen-year-old boy who won an exhibition for Balliol College and left for Oxford in the fall of 1863.

Oxford may have been, as Newman said, a "fair city seated

among groves, green meadows, and calm streams", but in the early 1860's the streams of intellectual, artistic, and religious thought were full of strong currents, cross-currents, and eddies.

It was such an environment as would have made strong appeals to the intellectually and artistically precocious youth we have seen at Highgate. On a young man of Hopkins' temperament and inclinations the milieu must have forced decisions which otherwise might have been delayed. The story of his undergraduate days could be written in terms of the major conflicts of Victorian ideologies, for we see Hopkins moving among the various schools of thought and making his own choices and drawing his own conclusions. But such a story must be generally told in negative terms, in terms of his rejections of several divergent ways of looking at life until in his last year at Oxford comes the great affirmation, his conversion to Catholicism.

To one who examines carefully his Oxford note-books, diaries, and letters, one general impression is immediately evident: the independence with which he moved among the various camps, the willingness to examine the tenets of opposing parties, the seriousness and eagerness with which he pursued a solution for his problems and the problems of his age. One of the finest general portraits of Hopkins comes from the pen of one who, looking back forty-five years, records that he talked with Hopkins only once, but still:

> At this moment, looking back over forty years, I seem to be gazing upon some great portrait of a face. What high serenity, what firm and resigned purpose, and withal what tranquil sadness or perhaps seriousness, suffusing the features rather than casting a shadow on them! I have no likeness, but I continue to see the face.... Of all I came across at Oxford, there was not one whose superfineness of mind and character was more expressed in his entire bearing.[2]

There were two major streams flowing through Oxford in the 'sixties. One was the spirit of Rationalism in religion, counteracted by a new renaissance of Tractarianism, the other was the growing aesthetic movement. To these main streams other minor brooks were tributaries.

The essence of the aesthetic movement is that beauty is made the supreme end and object of life and is erected into a religion. The direction of this pursuit of beauty was, to one living in the 1860's, not as easy to determine as it is to one looking back over the entire vista of the nineteenth century; further, the extremes (and at the same time the logical flowering) of the movement were not evident until the 'nineties, when the seed sown in the *Germ*, the Pre-Raphaelite journal of the 'fifties, culminated in the *Yellow Book*.

Although Ruskin was not to deliver his inaugural address in the Sheldonian Theatre as Slade professor of art until 1870, it was he who aroused a new interest in the beauty of the past by his publication of successive volumes of *Modern Painters* (1843–60). Moreover, he had, in 1851, defended with his genius the Pre-Raphaelites who were trying to create a beauty, old and yet new.

The aestheticism of Keats—especially that part which looked to the Middle Ages—found an expression in the formation, in 1848, of the Pre-Raphaelite Brotherhood, a band of artists, whose chief representative was Dante Gabriel Rossetti. In him romanticism is dissociated from religious faith, while the trappings of the Middle Ages are appreciated for their aura of beauty, and religion itself is regarded primarily from an aesthetic point of view.

William Morris, a disciple of Ruskin, studied under Rossetti for two years and in his *Defence of Guenevere* (1858) placed his poems in an atmosphere of wistful and nostalgic mediaevalism. The attempt of Ruskin, the Pre-Raphaelites, and Morris to recapture the Middle Ages by merely imitating its externals, by divorcing art from religion, accelerated the aesthetic movement, although both Ruskin and Morris partially saved themselves by later becoming social philosophers, and Ruskin had never in fact divorced art from morality.

When we approach the very pertinent problem of trying to discover how far Hopkins was interested in the tenets of these men and how far he was influenced or moulded by them, our difficulties are great because of the paucity of materials. But two things are clear: that he was interested in them and that he finally rejected them.

We know that he read *Modern Painters*. In his diary, he jotted down the names of the members of the Brotherhood; in the summer of 1864 he was introduced to some of them and spoke with them. He probably saw Rossetti's mural, Sir Launcelot's Vision of the Grail, on the walls of the Oxford Union. We know he was attracted by the "Blessed Damozel" and once tried his own hand at writing a Pre-Raphaelite ballad.

But the influence of Ruskin and the Pre-Raphaelites is most

easily perceptible in his drawings. Two books were filled with sketches—chiefly of landscapes, trees, and leaves—during his Balliol years. His note-books are filled with sketches of details of mediaeval churches he visited and with precise descriptions of ecclesiastical architecture—all in the manner of Ruskin. But Hopkins never could do what Ruskin and the Pre-Raphaelites did: he could never, in all his interest in the mediaeval, divorce art from religion.

One of the last things Hopkins wished to do before he entered the Jesuit novitiate in 1868 was to write for publication an essay summing up his final evaluation of the "mediaeval school of poets" with the recent appearance of Morris' *Earthly Paradise* as its central subject. We may presume from what we know of Hopkins' mind at that time that he would have found Morris' paradise indeed an earthly paradise.

But within the walls of Oxford itself were two men who were increasingly bringing their influence upon the minds and sensibilities of those who knew or heard them: Matthew Arnold and Walter Pater.

From 1857 to 1867 Arnold held the Chair of Poetry. Arnold was a new variation of the aesthete because he attacked traditional religion directly, affirming that men must live by its poetry and reject its metaphysics, theology, and dogma—an opinion shared by Ruskin. Already in Arnold's essay on Spinoza, published in the first series of his *Essays in Criticism*, a volume which Hopkins read, his contentions had been such. *St. Paul and Protestantism*, *Literature and Dogma*, and *God and the Bible* were not to be written till the 'seventies.

While there was much that was noble in Arnold's teaching, there was much more that pointed the way to Walter Pater and even to Oscar Wilde. The man who could write, "Most of what now passes with us for religion and philosophy will be replaced by poetry", is one, as T. S. Eliot not unfairly remarks, who would set up culture and beauty in the place of Christianity and religion.

Pater had been made a Fellow of Brasenose in 1864, and Hopkins came to know him personally, for Pater was one of his tutors and a separate note-book entitled "Essays for W. H. Pater" is extant. Hopkins also took notes on some lectures that Pater was giving on Greek philosophy. Some measure of Pater's regard for his young student can be seen in a letter Hopkins wrote to a friend during a summer vacation: "I have no plans till some time in

August, when Pater is going to ask me down to Sidmouth"—a
regard which must have been great, as Pater's biographer tells
us that one so withdrawing was loth to ask a student to join him in
the vacation[3]. But even ten years after leaving Oxford we find
Hopkins writing to Robert Bridges: "It was pleasing and flatter-
ing to hear that Mr. Pater remembers and takes an interest in
me."[4] Hopkins always retained a certain affection for his tutor,
and later in his Jesuit life when he was stationed at St. Aloysius'
Church in the university town he saw a good deal of his old don.

It is not difficult to discover what Pater was formulating during
the years that Hopkins was an undergraduate at Oxford, for his
essay on Winckelmann which was to appear in his *Renaissance*
(1873) had been written in 1868; what was to be the notorious
"Conclusion" was written in the same year. The philosophy he held
during his early years as Fellow developed logically into his better
known ethic of Cyrenaic intensity. However intellectualized and
refined was his gospel of hedonism, at heart it preached beauty
and pleasure as the goal of life. In his famous "Conclusion" he
stood for an ethic as well as an aesthetic: the highest wisdom,
said he, is the most passionate living, and

> Of such wisdom, the poetic passion, the desire for beauty, the
> love of art for its own sake, has most. For art comes to you pro-
> posing frankly to give nothing but the highest quality to your
> moments as they pass, and simply for those moments' sake.

Such a gospel of intensity would seem, as Pater's latest critic
has noted, a natural growth of romanticism, of the Keatsian
longing for a "Life of Sensations rather than of Thoughts".

Whenever Pater has anything good to say of religion, it is of
religion as art. Indeed in his later years Pater became something
of a ritualist. He separated, as did the whole aesthetic movement,
art and religion. Indeed he is said to have remarked that but for
its ritual the Church of England meant nothing to him. T. S.
Eliot has called his most mature work, *Marius*, "a prolonged
flirtation with the liturgy".

That Pater's philosophy must have attracted one side of the
temperament of the young Hopkins can hardly be doubted. In
"The Child in the House" Pater had said of Florian, a portrait of
himself, that "he was marked with more than customary sensuousness, 'the lust of the eye' as the Preacher says, which might
lead him, one day, how far!" Hopkins as well might have written

this of his earlier self and possibly an early realization—in fact we have seen some consciousness of this in his acts of denial and discipline at Highgate—had brought him to react against the hedonistic side of Pater's philosophy of art and of life.

Pater had written, in 1864, of the problem of one who pursues beauty:

> He may live, as Keats lived, a pure life; but his soul, like that of Plato's false astronomer, becomes more and more immersed in sense, until nothing which lacks the appeal to the sense has interest for him. How could such an one ever again endure the greyness of the ideal or spiritual world? . . . Christian asceticism . . . discrediting the slightest touch of sense, has from time to time provoked into strong emphasis the contrast or antagonism to itself, of the artistic life, with its inevitable sensuousness.

Of such a difficulty Hopkins was apparently aware, for we shall see the young Oxonian, under the impetus of religious asceticism, choosing the way of renunciation of the senses. Pater's view of Christian asceticism was a mistaken one, and one which Hopkins apparently shared for a time during his undergraduate days. It is a mistake that is not uncommon.

The results of his choice can be quickly seen in the difference between his Highgate and his Oxford poetry: how he reacted violently against his early sensuousness, thrust aside the pursuit of natural beauty, and suppressed the indulgence of the eye and ear. When we turn over the pages of his Oxford papers and read his verses we must, in fairness, recall that they survive largely by mistake. The poems which are extant from this period Hopkins thought he had destroyed in 1868; how much he destroyed we have no means of telling. What did survive, with the exception of a few pieces, is in his Oxford diary in an uncertain state: many are merely drafts and even the order of stanzas is uncertain. But as we turn the pages we shall find that the Oxford poetry is disappointing. While the metric is tidy and competent, the imagery lacks the precision of his earlier verse and too often we read merely the metrical rendering of prose ideas. Rare indeed is the revelling in nature found in his Highgate work; his lines do not fulfill the promise shown in his earlier "Vision of the Mermaids". To see how such a change was wrought we must turn to the development of his religious life as an undergraduate.

The Tractarian Movement, initiated in 1833 in reaction from the rationalism which had been undermining religion in the eighteenth century and more recently in the Oriel group of Noetics, lifted Oxford out of its early nineteenth-century lethargy. With the condemnation of Tract XC and the subsequent conversion of Newman, Tractarianism suffered widespread odium and the rationalists once more came into their day of triumph.

One who was himself concerned in the succeeding defence of orthodoxy, looking back, wrote:

> The influence of Newman, and in his own way of Pusey also, during the twelve years between 1833 and 1845 did not a little to check this spirit of Rationalism, and to prepare the Church to resist it if it should grow stronger. Many of the ablest and most highly cultured minds found refuge from this tendency in the fuller restatement of the whole Catholic creed which the Tractarians set before them; and it was a common saying when the Heads of the Houses were taking their measures against Newman, "You may crush Tractarianism, but then you will have to deal with Germanism." This was very soon found to be true. After the Academical overthrow of the Tractarians as a party in 1845, and the consequent suspicion and discredit which fell on them, a new and more vigorous school of Liberal Theologians began to gain a wider influence in Oxford.

Now it is important to understand just what this rationalism is if we are to understand one of the most important streams of thought in the Oxford of Hopkins' day. Rationalism is the very logical development of the principles of Protestantism whereby "human reason" is set up as the sole source and test of all truth. Cardinal Newman defined it in terms of "liberalism" when he said:

> By Liberalism I mean false liberty of thought, or the exercise of thought upon matters in which, from the constitution of the human mind, thought cannot be brought to any successful issue. . . Liberalism is the mistake of subjecting to human judgment those revealed doctrines which are in their nature beyond and independent of it, and claiming to determine on intrinsic grounds the truth and value of propositions which rest for their reception simply on the external authority of the Divine Word.

From within the walls of Oxford, in 1855, came a work strongly influenced by German rationalism which had been applying its criticism to the tenets of orthodox Christian faith as found and expressed in the Bible. This volume, Professor Jowett's edition of

St. Paul's Epistles, was accompanied by a series of notes in which the doctrine of atonement and its corollary of original or imputed sin was questioned. Undergraduates were reading Renan's *Life of Jesus* and Strauss' *Life of Christ*.

Essays and Reviews (1860) brought controversy once more within the Oxford colleges. This work by a group of critical rationalists, attacking the Bible as a standard of faith, contained essays by Frederick Temple, Rowland Williams, Baden Powell, Henry Bristow Wilson, C. W. Goodwin, Mark Pattison, and Benjamin Jowett. The last-named filled nearly a fourth of the volume with a long study, "On the Interpretation of Scripture", which the author had intended to form a part of a new edition of his St. Paul. The essay with its denial of supernatural inspiration of the Bible proved one of the most destructive in the *Essays and Reviews*. Mark Pattison contributed "Tendencies of Religious Thought in England, 1688–1750", which in effect was an enthusiastic eulogy of the rationalism of that period.

The sensation created by the collection of essays was very great. Two of the seven contributors, Rowland Williams and H. B. Wilson, were prosecuted in the ecclesiastical courts, although the Privy Council finally decided in their favour.

Dr. Jenkyns, Master of Balliol, considered Jowett's teaching "not only inconsistent with Anglican doctrines, but inconsistent with Christianity", and Jowett was deprived for ten years of the emoluments of his office as Regius Professor of Greek. The condemnation of his views proved the turning point of his life, for he left theological controversy in favour of his great translation of Plato.

Such was the condition of rationalism when Gerard Manley Hopkins came up to Balliol—and Balliol was a stronghold of liberalism—in the autumn of 1863. He came into contact, through personal relationship and reading, with its leaders.

It is difficult to determine to what extent the young Hopkins was influenced by these movements. His was a mind which, as we have seen in his relationships to the protagonists of a religion of beauty (for Ruskin, Arnold, and Pater, seeing the futility of rationalism, turned to art), apparently watched and studied the forces about him. Hopkins had come to Oxford from a moderately High Church family. But for a short time at Oxford he was swayed by the forces of opposition. One of his college friends wrote, "He was at first a little tinged with the liberalism prevalent among reading men.... All changed after his first confession to Liddon".[5]   That would indicate that his "tinge" lasted no more than a year, for he had gone up to Balliol in October, 1863, and was confessing to Liddon in November, 1864.

Jowett once said that to have formed the mind of a single person is no inconsiderable result of a life. But Jowett, who was not to become Master of Balliol till 1870, in spite of his great influence on the students in the college, was to have little permanent effect on Hopkins. Yet he called Hopkins the Star of Balliol and referred to him—in 1867 Hopkins got a first in Greats —as one of the finest Greek scholars he had ever seen at that college.

That the undergraduate examined the position of the rationalist school we cannot doubt. He read Jowett's *Epistles of St. Paul* and jotted down *Essays and Reviews* on his list of books to be read; he wrote out extracts from Mark Pattison's *Essays*. He took notes on lectures by Rowland Williams and wrote essays for him as his tutor. And Williams, too, had a high opinion of Hopkins' scholarship.

But as he turned upon the aesthetic movement, so he also turned upon Oxonian liberalism. The High Church Party had been active in reasserting the validity of faith. In fact its leader, Dr. Pusey, Newman's early companion in the Tractarian Movement, was looking Romeward once more. In 1865 he published his *Eirenicon*, the contents of which are indicated by the subtitle, "The Church of England, a Portion of Christ's One Holy Catholic Church, and a Means of Restoring Visible Unity". It represented the extravagances in belief and devotion current among Catholics as an important barrier to reunion with Rome.

Shortly after the *Eirenicon*, Pusey republished Tract XC, which had been Newman's last attempt to stay in the Anglican Church by interpreting the Thirty-nine Articles in as Catholic a sense as possible. Some measure of the position of the High Church party can be determined by the comparatively little excitement caused by the reissue of a document which some twenty-three years before had been vigorously condemned by the Heads of the Houses and had caused Newman to retire to Littlemore.

A second leader of the High Church party was busy within Oxford counteracting the negative criticisms of the rationalizing theologians, Henry Parry Liddon, who gathered large groups of students to hear his Bampton Lectures.

But soon after the turmoil caused by the publication of *Essays and Reviews* and at the same time as Dr. Pusey was attempting to find the fullness of faith, with all of its implications, in the Established Church, Newman published his famous *Apologia*, which tells the story of his reaction against the rationalism of the Oriel Noetics, his championing of the Tractarian cause, his growing dissatisfactions with the Via Media, his contention that there is "no medium in true philosophy, between Atheism and Catholicity", and his final realization and faith that only in Rome were to be found all solutions.

The publication of the *Apologia* in 1864 brought a renaissance of his reputation and influence, and a stream of converts began to flow Romewards again. His biographer, Wilfrid Ward, says, "It awoke from the dead the great memory of John Henry Newman whom the English world at large appeared to have forgotten. Those from whom the spell of his presence and words, felt in their youth at Oxford, had never passed away, now spoke out to a generation which knew him not".

Two years after the publication of the *Apologia* Newman wrote his "Letter to Dr. E. B. Pusey on his recent Eirenicon", a letter reprinted in 1870 along with a reprint of *Difficulties of Anglicans*. In it he reaffirmed the full doctrine of the Catholic Church and carefully took up Dr. Pusey's charges of extravagance in devotion, showing that what Dr. Pusey objected to was the flowering and fully developed expression of what Anglicans themselves, to be consistent, must hold.

Hopkins knew the leaders of the High Church party and was active in evaluating their position. He became a devoted follower of Dr. Pusey; Canon Liddon he knew even better and adopted him as his confessor. Some measure of their intimacy may be learned from lines in a letter which the latter wrote when Hopkins was about to be received by Newman: "After our intimate friendship with each other, I cannot bear to be silent, even though you should not be willing to listen."[6] How great was Canon Liddon's influence among undergraduates is indicated by a paragraph in one of the issues of the *Theological Review* in the 'sixties:

In the reaction which is undoubtedly taking place against Liberal opinions among the younger students at Oxford, Mr. Liddon stands out by common consent of all as the man who has had the greatest sway. He exercises a personal open influence such as has not been known at Oxford since the days when the Heads of Houses were alarmed because the undergraduates flocked in troops to attend Mr. Newman's lectures at St. Mary's. ... What Newman was to the men of his time in his University, that is Mr. Liddon to those of the present.

A wide circle of friends surrounded Hopkins at Oxford; many of them were strong in their High Church leanings; William Edward Addis, who later wrote of Hopkins, "I knew him in his undergraduate days far better than anyone else did", was one of them When Addis was received into the Catholic Church, Hopkins wrote to Newman: "Addis's loss will be a deep grief to Dr. Pusey, I think: he has known him so long and stayed with him at Chale in a retreat."[7] His friends Alfred William Garrett and Alexander Wood were also to leave Dr. Pusey for Rome. William Alexander MacFarlane was to be ordained, in 1866, as an Anglican priest.

Another intimate friend of Hopkins, V. S. S. Coles, a close friend of Canon Liddon also, was to become one of the leading High Churchmen of his generation. Coles had come to Balliol from Eton—"pre-eminent for his precocious theological bent and devotion to the *cause*"—where he had been the leader of a Puseyite group of which Digby Dolben and Robert Bridges were members.

Even one later to be so secular as Robert Bridges had come to Oxford with letters of introduction to Dr. Pusey and Canon Liddon and had expected to take orders.

Although Digby Dolben, whose life should be read in Robert Bridges' memoir, never took up residence at Oxford, Hopkins was greatly attracted to this fervently religious and artistic youth when he visited Bridges at Oxford in 1865. Gifted, sensitive, and emotional, Dolben had been almost extravagant in his religious ardour. That he intended to become a Catholic is quite clear, but he was drowned in 1867. The spirit of the impetuous youth lived in Hopkins' memory for many years.

We have one very amusing portrait of Hopkins during his Anglican days in a novel of Oxford undergraduate life written by one of Hopkins' acquaintances, Edmund Geldart, who later left the Church of England for Unitarianism. Some fifteen years after he left Oxford, Geldart wrote his witty and amusing novel, *A Son of Belial* (Balliol); it is frequently malicious and not necessarily reliable. Hopkins appears under the name of Gerontius Manley, "my ritualistic friend":

Gerontius Manley and I had many talks on religion. He was quite at one with me on the hollowness of Protestant orthodoxy, but he had a simple remedy—the authority of the Church. The right of private judgment must in the long run inevitably lead to Rationalism, as historically it has done.... He induced me to come with him to Canon Parry's tea-and-toast-and-testament. Canon Parry [Henry Parry Liddon] was, I believe, his father confessor, and the idol of the few Ritualists we had at Belial. About three hundred undergraduates used to assemble in the hall of Ann's to hear him expound the Greek Testament on a Sunday evening.

Even here there is no implication that Hopkins was a mere ritualist, as Pater afterwards became. Now ritualism has nothing in it to be condemned unless it dissociates liturgy from what it signifies, unless it pursues mere symbology in the spirit of aestheticism. Hopkins was too far-seeing to do that.

Indeed he was wrestling with the problems of the Elizabethan Settlement and trying to justify his adhesion to the Established Church. He was reading such books as Howard Broadley's *Christians of St. Thomas* and William Gresley's *Short Treatise on the English Church*, and he was carefully studying *Tracts for the Times* in an endeavour to vindicate his position as an Anglican.

Behind the religious verses of his Anglican days at Oxford (only one poem, "St. Dorothea", survives his Catholic days at Balliol) lies a severe asceticism. But this is seen also in numerous passages in his diaries and note-books, and the following is merely a representative passage:

> For Lent. No puddings on Sundays. No tea except if to keep me awake and then without sugar. Meat only once a day. No verses in Passion week or on Fridays. Not to sit in armchair except can work no other way. Ash Wednesday and Good Friday bread and water.[8]

The effects of such resolutions can be seen in such poems as "Easter Communion" (1865) and "Easter" (1866). Many of the themes of his undergraduate religious poetry we should expect from a young man full of regret for imperfections, desirous of peace, eager for certainty. But the most frequent theme tells us much about the ascetic strain which we saw in his refusal to make earthly beauty the goal of life. We saw this operating even in his school days when he was determined to master his senses and himself. Such a poem—or fragment—as "A Voice from the World" indicates the difficulties of renunciation. Occasionally there is a sensitive awareness of the attractiveness of the world:

> Once it was scarce perceivèd Lent
> For orience of the daffodil;
> Once, jostling thick, the bluebell sheaves
> The peacock'd copse were known to fill;
>
> .   .   .   .   .
>
> I walk towards eve our walks again;
> When lily-yellow is the west,
> Say, o'er it hangs a water-cloud
> And ravell'd into strings of rain.[9]

But the predominant note is:

> How shall I search, who never sought?
> How turn my passion-pastured thought
> To gentle manna and simple bread?[10]

The difficulty of the artist and the religious takes an enigmatic form; the sensuous beauty of the world attracts the artist: Hopkins' undergraduate note-books are filled with notations of one keenly sensitive to natural beauty, of one anxious to translate into words his awareness of shape, texture, colour; on the other hand, his religious asceticism makes him reject the senses. And the deficiencies of his undergraduate poetry, both secular and religious, may largely be told in terms of this conflict.

One of the most effective of these poems is "The Habit of Perfection", in which he is so conscious of what must be renounced that his love for the beauties of the earth flows over into the poetry. The poem consists of seven four-line stanzas in which he admonishes each of his senses to shut out the world. To his eyes he says:

> Be shellèd, eyes, with double dark
> And find the uncreated light:
> This ruck and reel which you remark
> Coils, keeps, and teases simple sight.

To his sense of touch:

> O feel-of-primrose hands, O feet
> That want the yield of plushy sward,
> But you shall walk the golden street
> And you unhouse and house the Lord.

The contrast with his Highgate poems is so direct that little comment is necessary. There is small evidence in his Oxford verses of the tyranny of the senses. It is almost as if he had written: "Oh for a life of sheer intellect, a life in which the senses play no part at all."

It was not until he was a Jesuit that he found a solution for this problem, and the remainder of the story of his Oxford days must be told in terms of his approach and conversion to Catholicism.

Of the actual thoughts which passed through his mind, of the motives, we know almost nothing; and it seems foolhardy to make conjectures. But it is very clear that his reception into the Catholic Church in October, 1866, was preceded by a fairly long preparation. Hopkins has sometimes been accused of making a hasty decision, but he did not. In the summer of 1864, after a year at Oxford, Hopkins was conscious of a Catholic strain in him; he said to one of his friends, "I have written three religious poems which however you would not at all enter into, they being of a very Catholic character".[11] He probably refers to "Barnfloor and Winepress", "New Readings", and "He hath abolished the Old Drouth". In his notebook they are followed by another poem, "Rest", expressing his desire for peace:

> I have desired to go
>   Where springs not fail;
> To fields where flies not the unbridled hail,
>   And a few lilies blow.
>
> I have desired to be
>   Where havens are dumb;
> Where the green water-heads may never come,
>   As in the unloved sea.[12]

And even in his essays for his tutor, Walter Pater, little indications of his leaning toward Catholicism appear, as where he says, in an unpublished essay entitled "The Pagan and Christian Virtues", that for the specifically Christian virtues "we look naturally to Catholicism, the consistent acceptation of philosophy".[13] In an essay on "The Origin of our Moral Ideas" he uses Thomas Aquinas as his authority.

In his note-book during the winter of 1865, he jotted down that he must read the life of Lacordaire—and Lacordaire was in a sense the model of liberals who found their way to Rome.

During the summer of 1865 he took a walking tour with his friend William Addis who wrote:

> When at Hereford we walked out to the Benedictine Monastery at Belmont and had a long conversation with Canon Raynal, afterwards abbot. I think he made a great impression on both of us and I believe that from that time our faith in Anglicanism was really gone.

And he goes on to give what may have been the reasons for Hopkins' final decision to join Rome:

> He [Canon Raynal] insisted that Anglican orders were at least of doubtful validity; that some grave and learned men questioned or denied their validity; and that this being so, it was unlawful till the doubt was cleared by competent authority to accept Anglican orders or even to participate in the Anglican Communion.[14]

He adds interestingly, "So far as I knew, Father Raynal was the first priest Hopkins had ever spoken to".

That fall, we know from his note-books, Hopkins entertained the thought of leaving the Anglican Church; and he also transcribed:

> Lead, Kindly Light, amid the encircling gloom
> Lead Thou me on!
> The night is dark, and I am far from home—
> Lead Thou me on!

—words which Newman had written when he was approaching a similar crisis in his own religious life. Indeed there is every reason to believe that Hopkins' path had been Newman's path, for he read *Difficulties of Anglicans* with great interest during his days at Oxford and years later he wanted to edit his *Grammar of Assent* with notes and a commentary.

But even during the Lent of 1866 Hopkins was deeply troubled and uncertain. In "Nondum" he is not trying to reason towards the existence of God, but he is searching for some manifestation of Him in the world about him, some indication that He expresses himself in a church:

> Yet know not how our gifts to bring,
> Where seek thee with unsandalled feet.

He seeks some indication of a creed in which He expresses Himself most fully:

> And Thou art silent, whilst Thy world
> Contends about its many creeds

And in anguish he prays for light:

> Speak! Whisper to my watching heart
> One word. . . .

That prayer was not to go unanswered.

His conversion belongs to July, 1866, and his reception to October of that year. All that we have genuine evidence for in reference to his conversion are his words, "When it came it was all in a minute". The words occur in a letter to a very close friend, the Rev. E. W. Urquhart, an Anglican priest, five years his senior, who was himself strongly drawn towards Rome; the letter is significant because it dismisses any pressure that may have been brought upon his decision:

> In fact as I told you my conversion when it came was all in a minute. Again I could not say that your talk influenced me in that direction: to see or hear "Romanising" things would throw me back on the English Church as a rule. In fact, it is almost implied by what I have told you that for a good time past I have been uninfluenced by anybody, especially from the Catholic side.[15]

Looking back and surveying his convictions, he wrote in another letter to the same friend:

> Although my actual conversion was two months ago yet the silent conviction that I was to become a Catholic has been present to me for a year perhaps, as strongly, in spite of my resistance to it when it formed itself into words, as if I had already determined it.[16]

It was not until six weeks after Hopkins' conviction was firm that he wrote his first letter to Newman, dated 28th August, 1866, to arrange with the great Oratorian at Birmingham an interview to ask advice and to be received. In part he wrote:

> I am anxious to become a Catholic. . . . I do not want to be helped to any conclusions of belief, for I am thankful to say my mind is made up, but the necessity of becoming a Catholic (although I have long foreseen where the only consistent position would lie) coming on me suddenly has put me into painful confusion of mind about my immediate duty in my circumstances. I

wished also to know what it would be morally my duty to hold on certain formally open points, because the same reasoning which makes the Tractarian ground contradictory would almost lead one also to shrink from what Mr. Oakley calls a minimizing Catholicism.... You will understand that by God's mercy I am clear as to the sole authority of the Church of Rome.[17]

The correspondence of Hopkins and Newman during this period of transition should be read in full because it characterizes both of them: the firmness of Hopkins, eager to become a Catholic no matter what the cost, the gentle kindness and understanding of Newman, anxious to make the difficult transition as smooth as possible. To Robert Bridges, from whom he had kept his conversion a secret, Hopkins wrote a long letter reporting the first meeting with Newman. Excerpts from it indicate something of the mind and character of Newman:

> Dr. Newman was most kind, I mean in the very best sense, for his manner is not that of solicitous kindness, but genial and almost, so to speak, unserious. And if I may say so, he was so sensible. He asked questions which made it clear for me how to act; I will tell you presently what that is: he made sure I was acting deliberately and wished to hear my arguments; when I had given them and said I cd. see no way out of them, he laughed and said "Nor can I" ... in no way did he urge me on, rather the other way.... More than once when I offered to go he was good enough to make me stay talking.... It is needless to say he spoke with interest and kindness and appreciation of all that Tractarians reverence.... I am to go over from Oxford to the Oratory for my reception next term—early in the term I must make it, and since a Retreat is advisable for a convert, Dr. Newman was so very good as to offer me to come there at Xtmas....[18]

Then the young man, not yet received into the Church, wrote to inform his parents of his conversion; their reaction is told in a letter of Hopkins to Newman—a letter direct and simple, and charged with the pain which only a convert can know:

> I have been up at Oxford just long enough to have heard from my father and mother in return for my letter announcing my conversion. Their answers are terrible: I cannot read them twice. If you will pray for them and me just now I shall be deeply thankful.[19]

Hurriedly, his father, Manley Hopkins, wrote to Liddon

to ask him to stop his son from going over to Rome. In rapid succession Liddon wrote a series of four letters, dated October 18th, 19th, 20th (1866), urging delay, reconsideration, and consultation. He suggested that Hopkins had been influenced by some of his friends (indeed the exact reverse was true if one of Hopkins' letters to Newman is reliable). He considered the step a blind one, and he accused Hopkins of being "under the impression that you have had a call from heaven . . . that you have had a special visitation of the grace of Our Lord. . . . Do have the courage—to stop—even now . . . you ought to rest on something more solid than the precarious hypothesis of a personal illumination".[20]

Catholics, like Father Lahey, cannot help calling the final affirmation, "By God's mercy I am clear as to the sole authority of the Church of Rome", to use Hopkins' words, by any other name than faith. Reason leads us to the very door of faith, but it leaves us at the door. Faith itself is a grace; the matter is best expressed in the words of the Vatican Council: "Although the assent of faith is in no sense blind, yet no one can assent to the Gospel teaching in the way necessary for salvation without the illumination of the Holy Spirit, Who bestows on all a sweetness in believing and consenting to the truth."

The time had come for parting with some of his close and revered friends, and on 18th October Newman wrote: "It is not wonderful that you should not be able to take so great a step without trouble and pain."[21] On the same day Hopkins received a curt and almost bitter note from one who had been his respected advisor, from Dr. Pusey, so distressed whenever a friend left him for Rome. He was, as Pius IX is said to have remarked, like a great church-bell which is for ever ringing others inside but itself remaining outside. On 21st October, 1866, Hopkins came inside.

During this last of his years at Balliol, Hopkins must have looked at Oxford very much with the same eyes as did Charles Redding, the central figure in Newman's *Loss and Gain: The Story of a Convert*:

> Whatever he was to gain by becoming a Catholic, this he had lost; whatever he was to gain higher and better, at least this and such as this he never could have again. He could not have another Oxford, he could not have the friends of his boyhood and youth in the choice of his manhood.

Hopkins was busy healing the breach with his family, reading hard for Greats, and trying to determine whether he had a vocation for the priesthood, a consideration which became uppermost in his mind soon after he became a Catholic. For almost two years he was weighing carefully this possibility before he finally entered the Jesuit novitiate.

Between terms, in January, 1867, he made a retreat and spent some time at Birmingham with Newman, who urged him not to hurry his decision.

It is significant that the man who had seen little of him before this visit—perhaps only a few hours—offered him a position at the Oratory School. After Hopkins had taken a double first in Greek in the Trinity term at Oxford, he went to Birmingham on 13th September, 1867, as a Master at the Oratory school conducted by Newman.

But after Christmas he did not return to the Oratory, because he was so anxious to settle his future. To Robert Bridges on 9th January, 1868, just after he himself had left the school and as Bridges was about to leave for a long trip to the continent, Hopkins wrote of his impending decision:

> The year you will be away I have no doubt will make a great difference in my position though I cannot know exactly what. But the uncertainty I am in about the future is so very unpleasant and so breaks my powers of applying to anything that I am resolved to end it, which I shall do by going into a retreat at Easter at the latest and deciding whether I have a vocation to the priesthood.[22]

That retreat was made at the Benedictine Monastery which Hopkins had visited three years before—with Father Raynal who was the first Catholic priest Hopkins had ever known; and now he resolved to take orders.

For a year and a half he had been considering the Catholic priesthood; how seriously he considered becoming a Benedictine we do not know. Just how his decision to enter the Society of Jesus was reached we have no hint, but in May, 1868, Newman congratulated him:

> I am both surprised and glad at your news . . . I think it is the very thing for you. You are quite out in thinking that when I offered you a home here, I dreamed of your having a vocation for us. This I clearly saw you had *not*, from the moment you came to

us. Don't call "the Jesuit discipline" hard; it will bring you to heaven. The Benedictines would not have suited you.

We all congratulate you.

Ever yours affectionately,

John H. Newman [23]

Thus was answered the prayer Newman had made in October, 1866, before Hopkins' reception: "You have my best prayers that He who has begun the good work in you may finish it—and I do not doubt He will."[24]

On 7th September, 1868, he entered Manresa House, the Jesuit Novitiate at Roehampton, just outside London. He was about to translate into action the substance of one of his Oxford poems:

> And other science all gone out of date
> And minor sweetness scarce made mention of:
> I have found the dominant of my range and state—
> Love, O my God, to call Thee Love and Love.[25]

Ad Majorem Dei Gloriam

MANRESA, the Jesuit novitiate which Gerard Manley Hopkins now entered, is appropriately named after the cave, not far from Barcelona, in which St. Ignatius, founder of the Society of Jesus, formulated his famous Spiritual Exercises, the epitome of Jesuit spirituality. Shortly before Hopkins left for Manresa, Newman had written: "Don't call 'the Jesuit discipline' hard: it will bring you to heaven." We must now see in what the training and discipline of a Jesuit consist.

The young novice spends his first two years in deep seclusion and constant prayer. St. Ignatius ruled that study, except perhaps in the second year, be on the whole excluded in order that the future religious might devote himself to the spiritual life. The routine of the novice consists of attending mass, meditation, reading spiritual books, conferring with the directors, and performing such menial tasks as housework and gardening.

After two years of this training, the novice takes his first vows, and, being now formed to self-renunciation, is permitted to pursue his studies. "After", says the founder, "the foundation of self-denial has been laid in the souls of those who are admitted amongst us, it will be time to build up the edifice of knowledge." Hence the years that immediately follow are devoted to the study of literature, the classics, mathematics, history, and philosophy. Duties of teaching may intervene. Then comes a period of three or four years devoted to the study of theology, after which the scholastic receives the orders of priesthood. Then the Jesuit enters upon an active ministry, which may consist of preaching, teaching, or any office in which his superiors think him most likely to contribute to the object of the Society, the greater glory of God.

But St. Ignatius is not yet satisfied. After a few years as an active priest in the world, the Jesuit returns for a second novitiate, his "tertianship", and is told once more to cast aside all study, and, as in the first days of his religious life, to devote himself to prayer and self-examination. During this last and final year of probation the founder directs the religious to exercise himself "in schola affectus" (the school of the heart). Then the final vows crown the legislation which governs the long and strenuous formation of the member of the Society of Jesus.

As all Jesuits go through this long training, so did Gerard Manley Hopkins. He was a novice from 1868 to 1870, when he took his first vows and started three years of philosophical studies at St. Mary's Hall, Stonyhurst (1870–73). For a year he went back to Manresa House to teach classics. Then he left for St. Beuno's College in North Wales for three years of theology. In 1877 he was ordained Then for four years he served in various capacities, mostly as parish priest and preacher, at London, Chesterfield, Oxford, and Liverpool, until in 1881 he entered his Tertianship. After teaching Latin and Greek at Stonyhurst for two years (1882–4) he held the Chair of Greek at University College, Dublin, until his death in 1889.

On 18th September, 1868, he noted in his journal, "The Long Retreat began". His life as a novice for the next two years was to be given to spiritual training, especially by the use of the Spiritual Exercises. Reminding us that all novices make the spiritual exercises for thirty days very shortly after they enter the order, Father Pollen remarks that this is really the chief test of a vocation, as it is also in epitome the main work of the two years of novitiate and for that matter of the entire life of a Jesuit. On these exercises the Constitutions, the life, and the activity of the Society are based, so that they are really the chief factor in forming the character of a Jesuit.

It is almost impossible to exaggerate the importance of the Spiritual Exercises in the life of a Jesuit. St. Ignatius had considered them the most important armour of his sons; the Constitutions of the Society urge their constant use. And recently Father LaFarge wrote of them: "The personal practice of the Spiritual Exercises is especially a perpetual means of regeneration. By means of them every Jesuit is reminded every year of his life of the primitive ideals of his Order."

For twenty-one years Hopkins dedicated himself to the Society of Jesus; for twenty-one years he studied, meditated, and practised the Spiritual Exercises. They became a part of his life and attitude. They gave direction to all he experienced, thought, and wrote. They influenced his most exuberant and joyous poems; they were part of his sufferings and desolation. He delivered sermons suggested by them, started to write a commentary on them; he gave them to others. They fashioned his reaction to nature and beauty. Their echo is found in his humility, his asceticism, in his scrupulousness, his consciousness of imperfection, in his abnega-

tion and in the integrity with which he faced hardship and disappointment. His attitude toward poetry and fame was shaped
by them. They moulded his native temperament and sensibility
to an ideal of perfection. Without knowing something of them we
can hardly know the priest-poet.

The Spiritual Exercises were conceived at a time when, looking
back on his past life, St. Ignatius analysed the struggles through
which he had passed in his conversion, and pondered over the
succession of events that had led his soul on its upward path.
Moved by God, he recorded the results of these experiences and
inspirations for the help and enlightenment of other souls strugg-
ling along the same road. Thus it is that the book was lived before
it was written; and it remains a book, as Father DeRavignan has
admirably expressed it, "not composed in order to be read, but in
order to be put into practice; and hence one cannot really appreciate it with any justice, until one has passed through the school
of experience".

It is not a book to be gone through alone, for it presupposes a
wise and experienced director. The book was not meant for
popular circulation; it was not intended to be a manual of devotion
like the *Imitation of Christ*, so loved by St. Ignatius. It was to be
put into the hands of those directing the exercises, as a guide for
giving them. Supplementary to the Exercises themselves is the
Directory, an official body of instructions for directors, drawn up
in the 1590's on the basis of notes by St. Ignatius and the experiences of others who had administered the exercises.

The purpose and meaning of the *Spiritual Exercises* has been
elaborated by St. Ignatius himself:

> By this name of Spiritual Exercises is meant every way of
> examining one's conscience, of meditating, of contemplating, of
> praying vocally and mentally, and of performing other spiritual
> actions, as will be said later. For as strolling, walking, and running
> are bodily exercises, so every way of preparing and disposing the
> soul to rid itself of all the disordered tendencies, and, after it is rid,
> to seek and find the Divine Will as to the management of one's life
> for the salvation of the soul, is called a Spiritual Exercise.

All those who apply for entrance into the Society are required,
during their probationary period, to make the Exercises to test
their vocation. Yet this guidebook to the spiritual life is not
limited to the purpose of testing a religious vocation, or confined

to the use of Jesuits. This is evident from a recent editor's outline of the purposes of the Exercises:

> To order one's life according to the will of God, that is the purpose which the retreatant is supposed to have in view. He comes into retreat either to consider the question of his vocation, whether it be the ordinary one in the world, or the priesthood, or the Religious state; or to reform if need be, and to order his life in a state already chosen and fixed; or simply to seek a renewal of fervour and to make progress in the life of grace.

The four parts into which the Exercises are divided are called Four Weeks, a name derived from the divisions of the month which they are supposed to fill. If the time is curtailed, the four divisions still retain the name of Weeks. Each Week has its special object and aim. A summary view is given in the *Directory:*

> The First Week comprises the consideration of sins, in order that we may come to know their foulness, and may truly hate them with due sorrow and purpose of amendment. The Second sets down before us the Life of Christ, in order to kindle in us an eager desire of imitating Him; and to make this imitation as perfect as possible there is set before us also the method of Election, that we may choose such a state of life as may be most in accordance with the will of God; or if we are not now free to make such a choice, some instructions are given for reforming our life in that state in which we are. The Third Week takes in the Passion of Christ, the contemplation of which begets pity, sorrow, and shame, and greatly inflames our desire of imitating Him. Lastly, the Fourth is concerned with the Resurrection of Christ and His glorious appearances, and with the favours bestowed on us by God, and other like matters which are calculated to kindle His love in our hearts.

The First Week is preceded by a sort of prolegomenon, the "Principle and Foundation", as it is called. It states the basic principles of the spiritual life, and upon it is based the whole superstructure of the Exercises. So often shall we refer to it and so central is it to an understanding of Gerard Manley Hopkins that we must carefully consider each word of it:

> Man was created to praise, reverence, and serve God, our Lord, and by this means to save his soul.
> And the other things on the face of the earth were created for man's sake, and in order to aid him in the prosecution of the end for which he was created.

Whence it follows, that man ought to make use of them just so far as they help him to attain his end, and ought to withdraw himself from them just so far as they hinder him.

It is therefore necessary that we should make ourselves indifferent to all created things in all that is left to the liberty of our free will, and is not forbidden; in such sort that we do not for our own part wish for health rather than sickness, for wealth rather than poverty, for honour rather than dishonour, for a long life rather than a short one, and so in all other things, desiring and choosing only that which may lead us more directly to the end for which we were created.

This is a statement of the essence of Ignatian and Christian asceticism: earthly things have a conditional value and are to be used only so far as they are serviceable for the attainment of the supreme and ultimate end; they are to be renounced in so far as they withdraw one from God and become ends in isolation. Yet it should be carefully noted—every phrase is of the utmost importance—that the "Principle and Foundation" in the last clause points beyond mere asceticism, beyond that half-way house of the spiritual life. Detachment is not enough, for beyond mere detachment, the soul, set free and transmuted by the Fire of Love, is to come to the yearning for positive identification with Christ, that loving desire to be an *alter Christus.*

The special objectives of the Four Weeks which now unfold before us have often been characterized as follows: the first, *deformata reformare;* the second, *reformata conformare;* the third, *conformata confirmare;* and the fourth, *confirmata transformare.* Now it will be seen that these are very like the traditional stages of the spiritual life which ascetical theologians always speak of, the purgative, illuminative, and unitive ways. Yet, the *Directory* warns us:

It would be a mistake if anyone were to suppose that having gone through the First Week he was perfectly and fully cleansed of sin; and after the Second and Third Weeks, perfectly illuminated; and at last, at the end of the Fourth Week, that he had attained to perfect union with God. For all these stages require much time and care and labour in rooting out faults, subduing passions and acquiring virtues.

But the First Week does have as its objective the rooting out of all sin and inordinate desire, the breaking down of the barriers between the soul and its Maker. Thus the *Directory* continues:

The First Week has a certain correspondence and analogy to the purgative way, since it is entirely occupied with reflections and considerations on past sins, and with exciting as great a sorrow and contrition for them as possible, and a fear of eternal punishment, so that the heart may be withdrawn from the love of every earthly thing, and established in hatred and detestation of sin. All which belongs to the purgation of the soul.

The Second, Third, and Fourth Weeks of the Spiritual Exercises are entirely positive, the training of the Christian to perfection after sin has been abandoned. Of these the Second is in many ways the most marvellous of all. Its specific object is to discover the degree of perfection to which Christ calls us.

The climax of the Second Week is the "Election", in which, after seeing just what it means to follow and imitate Christ in all things, and realizing that "he will benefit himself in all spiritual things in proportion as he goes out of his self-love, will, and interest", the exercitant, moved by the love of Christ and the desire to be like him in all things, elects and willingly embraces the perfection to which God calls him.

The Third Week, by its meditation on the Passion of Christ, is intended to confirm the exercitant in his resolutions, while the Fourth Week heartens him by seeing the glory of Christ's victory in which he will have part. It can be seen how the Second and Third Week correspond to the Illuminative, and the Fourth to the Unitive Way.

Crowning all, St. Ignatius added "The Contemplation to Gain Love", which is the final goal and climax of the entire Spiritual Exercises—the unitive way. Here all is transmuted by the Fire of Love. On man's part it is union through a self-sacrificing love in which he offers all he has to the Great Lover:

> Take, Lord, and receive all my liberty, my memory, my intellect, and all my will—all that I have and possess. Thou gavest it to me: to Thee, Lord, I return it! All is Thine, dispose of it according to all Thy will. Give me Thy love and grace, for this is enough for me.

On God's part it is a giving of himself to his creature, a communication with him not only directly, but also—this needs emphasis—through the beauty of this world.

None of the asceticism which St. Ignatius recommends is to be any more than a means to set man free for the exercise of love, to clear away the path to his one great goal, union with God through love.

Such then are the Spiritual Exercises which St. Ignatius made the centre of the life of every Jesuit. The story of Gerard Manley Hopkins from 1868, when he entered the Jesuit novitiate, till 1889 when he died is largely the story of the pervasive influence of the Spiritual Exercises upon him.

Unfortunately our knowledge of his personal life and intimate experiences during his first years in the Society is slender. For the period from his entrance till the early months of 1877 only half a dozen rather non-committal letters which he wrote to Robert Bridges—a man who was utterly unsympathetic to the religious life—were written. His correspondence with Richard Watson Dixon and with Coventry Patmore had not yet begun. There are a few miscellaneous letters to Edward Bond and Alexander Baillie. But on the whole these early years were silent ones, years given to the pursuit of a new ideal.

We have no poems to make clear his progression, for during the summer prior to his entrance into Manresa he made a voluntary holocaust of his verses, and gave up composition till 1875 when he wrote "The Wreck of the Deutschland".

But there is one very important source of information, his Journal. This extends from the summer of 1868, just prior to his entrance into the novitiate, up to February, 1875, when he had been at St. Beuno's for some five months. He apparently also kept a book in which he entered spiritual notes and meditations. It is clear that the extant Journal was intended for non-religious notes and meditations; an entry of 1873 reads, "August 30 –September 8—Retreat, of which there are notes in my meditation papers"; another jotting a year later remarks, "At night the retreat began, given by Fr. Coleridge. There are some remarks on it in my notes of meditation" [1] Unfortunately this second journal or diary has been destroyed or has disappeared. But there are a few hints about the trend of his religious thought and development which crept into his secular Journal.

This Journal is a remarkable note-book filled with a wide variety of interests. In it one will find his careful recordings of the way people around him pronounced words, of his walks alone or with fellow-novices, of visits from members of his family, of folk-lore that he collected, of pictures which he saw at the Kensington Museum or National Gallery, of sky and sea, clouds and comets, waves, waterfalls, gulls and swans, of trees and mountains.

His interest in the natural beauty of the world about him dominates all other interests. Nine-tenths of the Journal are filled with his notations of the radiance and splendour of objects of natural beauty. In all he endeavoured to set down (often including sketches in the margins) his observations precisely and exactly. The cumulative effect of reading the Journal is tremendous, for the fresh keenness and sensitiveness of one deeply attracted by every colour and form are on every page. There is an awareness of detail without a loss of the larger unity, there is exuberance without effusion. He even coined words—the Journal was meant for his eyes only—to record exactly what he saw and felt.

The impact of his religious life is in the Journal too, in spite of the fact that he tried to keep two separate diaries. The conscientiousness and sacrificing zeal with which Hopkins was training himself is clear in a passage embedded in a description of the beauty of Wales, where he was pursuing his theological studies at St. Beuno's. The entry indicates that he was trying to order all his choices and decisions in accordance with the rules for making an "election" in the Spiritual Exercises. According to St. Ignatius,

> In every good election, as far as depends on us, the eye of our intention ought to be simple, only looking at what we are created for, namely, the praise of God our Lord and the salvation of our soul. And so I ought to choose whatever I do, that it may help me for the end for which I am created.

After setting down with delicate precision the beauty of his new surroundings, the scholastic wrote:

> Looking all round but most in looking far up the valley I felt an instress and charm of Wales. Indeed in coming here I began to feel a desire to do something for the conversion of Wales. I began to learn Welsh too but not with very pure intentions perhaps. However on consulting the Rector on this, the first day of the retreat, he discouraged it unless it were purely for the sake of labouring among the Welsh. Now it was not and so I saw I must give it up. At the same time my music seemed to come to an end. Yet, rather strangely, I had no sooner given up these two things (which disappointed me and took an interest away—and at that time I was very bitterly feeling the weariness of life and shed many tears,

perhaps not wholly into the breast of God but with some unmanliness in them too, and sighed and panted to Him), I had no sooner given up the Welsh than my desire seemed to be for the conversion of Wales and I had it in mind to give up everything else for that; nevertheless weighing this by St. Ignatius' rules of election I decided not to do so.[2]

In addition to the firmness with which he was trying to apply the Spiritual Exercises to his own life, we must notice in this passage that he expresses a connection between the "instress and charm" of Wales ("instress" is a word he attached to the intensity of feeling and associations which something beautiful brought to him) and a desire to convert it to God. The relationship at this point is hardly definable.

Even more remarkable is a whole series of passages, scattered through the Journal, in which the experience of earthly beauty is accompanied by religious experience. These passages range from such notations as "Laus Deo—the river to-day and yesterday" and an experience of the heavens as "a new witness to God" to such an entry as this: "As we drove home the stars came out thick: I leant back to look at them and my heart opening more than usual praised our Lord to and in whom all that beauty comes home."[3]

This association of the experience of beauty with a religious experience becomes increasingly more and more central for Hopkins. In the above passages we have germinally the attitude which we shall see more explicitly developed in his mature poems. Never before in the work of Hopkins—in his Highgate poems, his Oxford diary, or his undergraduate verses—had he connected his sensitivity to the beauty of the world so closely with his religion.

How this emerging relationship was shaped and moulded by St. Ignatius and by Duns Scotus is not easily summed up, for first we must go back to examine a term which Hopkins coined to designate the principle of beauty in things: inscape. Nearly fifty times this word occurs in the Journal which Hopkins kept from 1868 to 1875. "All the world", he writes in one entry, "is full of inscape."[4] In another he reminds himself: "Unless you refresh the mind from time to time you cannot always remember or believe how deep the inscape in things is."[5] To all varieties of natural beauty he applies the term. Always "inscape" is applied to some particular thing of beauty which is distinctive and patterned.

Later in his letters he referred to inscape as "the very soul of

art",[6] "that is species or individually-distinctive beauty of style".[7]
In a famous letter to Robert Bridges he applied it to his own
poetry:

> No doubt my poetry errs on the side of oddness. . . . But as air,
> melody, is what strikes me most of all in music and design in paint-
> ing, so design, pattern or what I am in the habit of calling "inscape" is
> what above all I aim at in poetry. Now it is the virtue of design,
> pattern, or inscape to be distinctive and it is the vice of distinctive-
> ness to become queer. This vice I cannot have escaped.[8]

But that "inscape" meant much more than external design or
pattern is clear from passages in which the expression is connected with the inner kernel of being. In one of his sermons he
spoke of Satan as one "who had fallen through pride and self-love";
in a later essay he became more specific when he referred to
Lucifer's fall as "a dwelling on his own beauty, an instressing of
his own inscape, and like a performance on the organ and instrument of his own being".[9]

While the term, therefore, was used with some flexibility, the
variations in its application are largely a matter of emphasis:
sometimes he stresses "inscape" as configuration, design, shape,
pattern, and contour—the "outer form" of a thing; sometimes
he stresses "inscape" as the ontological secret behind a thing, as
the "inner form". But usually he employs the word to indicate
the essential individuality and particularity or "selfhood" of a
thing working itself out and expressing itself in design and pattern.
This he then calls beauty.

This conception of beauty as the essence or "inner form" of a
thing as expressed in sensible pattern and design or "outer form"
bears a remarkable analogy to the traditional scholastic description of beauty which Jacques Maritain has treated so well in *Art
and Scholasticism*. The schoolmen had called beauty "the splendour
of form shining on the proportioned parts of matter". "Form"
here must be understood in the philosophic sense as "the principle determining the peculiar perfection of everything which is,
constituting and completing things in their essence and their
qualities; the ontological secret, so to speak, of their innermost
being." Hopkins himself spoke of this with clarity and precision:
"It is certain that in nature outward beauty is the proof of inward
beauty. . . . Fineness, proportion, of feature comes from a moulding force which succeeds in asserting itself over the resistance of

cumbersome or restraining matter. . . . The moulding force, the life, is the form in the philosophic sense."[10]

Thus to have beauty, form must be found "shining on the proportioned parts of matter"; that is, the "inner form" must be expressed in "outer form". For as one of the modern Catholic philosophers, E. I. Watkin, has written in a sentence which might have been found in Hopkins' Journal: "The fact that outer form is apprehended by aesthetic intuition as the expression of an inner form, invests it as thus apprehended with that specific and irreducible quality we term beauty, which has been aptly defined as the 'splendor' or 'radiance of form'."

So strongly did Hopkins feel that "it is the virtue of . . . inscape to be distinctive", that the splendour of form shining on the proportioned parts of matter is "individually-distinctive", that when he opened the pages of a philosopher who justified this feeling, the young man was exultant. In 1872 he enthusiastically put in his Journal:

> After the examinations we went for our holiday out to Douglas in the Isle of Man Aug. 3. At this time I had first begun to get hold of the copy of Scotus on the Sentences in the Baddely library [Duns Scotus' commentary on the Sentences of Peter Lombard from the library at Stonyhurst, where Hopkins was studying, 1870-74] and was flush with a new stroke of enthusiasm. It may come to nothing or it may be a mercy from God. But just then when I took in any inscape of the sky or sea I thought of Scotus.[11]

This "new stroke of enthusiasm" became a hobby. "I walked with Herbert Lucas by the river and talked Scotism", he chronicles a year later. The next summer, 1874, he entered into his Journal:

> I met Mr. David Lewis, a great Scotist, and at the same time old Mr. Brande Morris was making a retreat with us: I got to know him, so that oddly I made the acquaintance of two and I suppose the only two Scotists in England in one week.[12]

And a year later, in the midst of strenuous theological studies at St. Beuno's, he answered a letter in which Bridges had expressed an enthusiasm for Hegel:

> It was with sorrow that I put back Aristotle's Metaphysics in the library some time ago feeling that I could not read them now

and so probably should never. After all I can, at all events a little,
read Duns Scotus and I care for him more even than Aristotle
and more *pace tua* than a dozen Hegels.[13]

To one who experienced form as highly distinctive and individual, the appeal of Scotus is not difficult to understand. But
we must be careful not to consider the influence of Scotus as too
positive an initiating force, for Hopkins had been using the word
"inscape" for almost four years before he took Scotus out of the
library. It was not that he found something he had not known.
He did not become a disciple of Scotus in the sense that a student
adopts the teachings of a master; rather, both of them had the
same experience of "form" as sharply individual and particular.
His reading of the mediaeval Franciscan tended to make him feel
that he was correct and that there was a philosophical justification
for his own analysis of beauty.*

The Scotist theories of individuation and of knowledge—we
shall see these constantly illustrated in his poems—would seem
to have offered intellectual justification to Hopkins the artist.
Much as Scotus' teachings gave to the artist, they gave no less to
Hopkins the religious.

"I do not think I have ever seen anything more beautiful than
the bluebell I have been looking at", enthusiastically wrote the
young novice in his Journal; and he added significantly, "I know
the beauty of our Lord by it. Its inscape is mixed of strength and
grace" [14] The artist was recording more than his experience of
the beauty or "inscape" of the bluebell; he was also signalizing a
religious experience in which the apprehension of "inscape"
played a part. It was as if he had concretely apprehended in the
warmth of his aesthetic intuition that, as St. Thomas said, the
beauty of creatures is nothing else than the likeness of the beauty
of God. Already we have seen some of the jottings which Hopkins
made after entering Manresa, when the experience of beauty was
accompanied by a lifting of heart and mind to God.

In many of his later poems this sacramental view of nature is
developed; in it the poet and the priest reach through the things
of sense to hidden beauties. The sacramental view enabled him
to cancel the lines he wrote in 1866:

> Be shellèd, eyes, with double dark
> And find the uncreated light,

* See Appendix, "Duns Scotus and Hopkins."

and in 1870 to write the passage on the bluebell. In the first poem he wrote as a Jesuit scholastic he exclaims:

> I kiss my hand
> To the stars, lovely-asunder
> Starlight, wafting him out of it.

While many of the mystics have closed their eyes the better to concentrate on the things of the spirit (the Curé d'Ars feared that even the sight of a rose would distract him), Hopkins opened them wide to find the One ablaze in the many.

Now Scotus was very forceful in the statement of a sacramental view of the world, for he contended that God created the world to make it possible for man to look upon the visible beauties of the universe and experience them as a bridge between the finite and the infinite. Individual "inscape", forms splendidly shining on matter, are images, similitudes, representations, analogues of Divine Ideas. The experience of the beauties of the world, of its "inscape", then, leads to Beauty, to God. Thus Scotus offered to Hopkins a very real justification for his love of inscapes.

Scotus taught Hopkins in still another way how to give his experience of beauty a supernatural value. This has been admirably treated in an article by W. W. H. Gardner in *Scrutiny* (June, 1936). Now, the aesthetic experience is an activity of man's individual nature, at the centre of which is the Scotist "haecceitas," the selfhood, in man identified with the will. By the exercise of the will man's nature is perfected in the moral sphere. By a volitional "act of love" his experience of beauty may be directed Godwards and affirmed in God so that it becomes a meritorious act. Thus Scotus taught Hopkins how "mortal beauty" may become for him supernatural, "God's better beauty, grace". We shall see many poems in which Hopkins concerns himself with directing beauty, by an act of love, to God; with an affirming beauty in God so that it may acquire for him an eternal value; with the problem of directing the personality so that its acts are crowned with grace.

But all of this inevitably brings us back to the Spiritual Exercises and to St. Ignatius who said, "If everything is directed towards God, everything is prayer". If Hopkins had read—as most young novices do—the standard biographies of the saint, he would have learned that his master "found no greater consolation than in looking up at the sky and stars, for in doing so, often and long, his soul was strangely impelled, as it were, to seek the service of God", and he would have read how St. Ignatius "beheld God Himself in His works, and from them drew a lesson of the intelligence, wisdom, power and glory of the Heavenly Artificer".

The affirming of beauty in God which Scotus urged is also the practical application of the "Principle and Foundation", in which man is exhorted to use all created things to attain to God. So, too, a sacramental view of the world which sees all creatures as avenues to Uncreated Being, there has its origin, and its culmination comes in the closing section of the Spiritual Exercises, the famous "Contemplation for Obtaining Love", where the exercitant contemplates "God our Lord . . . in every creature, according to His own essence, presence, and power".

The "Principle and Foundation" is both positive and negative. On the one hand, man must employ his sensitivity to beauty to lead him to God. On the other hand he must withdraw from beauty and the life of the senses in so far as they are not avenues to God. Created beauty must not be made into the end of man or of life, must not be made a religion, must not be deified. Now this implies the necessity of an asceticism and mortification which are often misunderstood. The purpose of asceticism is to free man from inordinate attachment—a discipline and purification of the senses, which emerge not suppressed but controlled. It is really only a preliminary and negative aspect of a very positive thing, a giving of due order to all things in terms of their respective degrees of goodness, truth, and beauty.

Hopkins disciplined his senses. We find him recording in his Journal soon after he entered the novitiate that "a penance which I was doing from January 25 to July 25 prevented my seeing much that half year". And when he did open his eyes he looked upon a new world.

The true spiritual odyssey, as Father G. Vann has pointed out, is that of Malachy, the Irish bishop: *spernere mundum, spernere sese, spernere nullum* (to despise the world, to despise thyself, to despise nothing at all). To one who has travelled through the Purgative Way "all creatures are pure to enjoy, for it enjoyeth all creatures in God, and God in all creatures", as Meister Eckhart so well stated the paradox. Creatures lose nothing of their beauty but are enhanced because they are enjoyed in and for God.

And such is the new vision of a new world which opens before the person who reaches the climax of the Spiritual Exercises, the

Contemplation to Obtain Love, and sees the love of God communicating itself to man through the beauty of the world about him.

Hopkins once wrote to his friend Dixon how deeply he was moved by Plato, who had "seen something", who had such a "spiritual insight into nature". And he must have been thinking of the marvellous passage in the *Phaedrus* where Plato tells how earthly beauty is a mirror of Eternal beauty, so that only he who has contemplated the Godhead can truly recognize it and "is amazed when he sees anyone having a godlike face or form, which is the expression of Divine Beauty; and at first a shudder runs through him, and the old awe steals over him". It is really only such as St. Francis of Assisi (we must not, of course, sentimentalize by forgetting his severe ascetical preparation) who can really relish the beauty of even this world.

Of this "spiritual insight into nature", Hopkins granted that "if we sort things, so that art is art and philosophy philosophy, it seems rather the philosopher's than the poet's" prerogative, yet he was prepared to defend it as "above all the poet's gift".[15] In Hopkins, we find united the philosopher and the poet.

But as we approach the study of the poems which Hopkins wrote, we come to the problem of the judgment of the work of art and we must be careful not to praise it for the wrong things. Its religious significance does not in itself give it poetic greatness; it may express a sacramental view of nature, and yet it may be an inferior poem. Whether it is art or not depends on artistic standards. "The standard and aim is strict beauty", Hopkins wrote to Bridges, "and if the writer misses that his verse, whatever its incidental merits, is not strict or proper poetry".[16] Hopkins expressed this in another way in saying that a work of art is "good" or less good, but as such is not right or wrong:

> Therefore this masterhood,
> This piece of perfect song,
> This fault-not-found-with good
> Is neither right nor wrong.
>
> .   .   .   .
>
> No more than Re and Mi,
> Or sweet the golden glue
> That's built for by the bee.

The poem from which these lines are taken, "On a Piece of Music" (an undated fragment), makes the important distinction which was maintained by the scholastic tradition—the distinction between art and prudence.* Maritain has carefully shown the importance of differentiating between the two, and here we can but follow his analysis. While art operates "ad bonum operis", for the good of the work done, prudence operates "ad bonum operantis", for the good of the worker. Art as such has no other end than the perfection of the work made, and not the perfection of the man making. That is the view that Hopkins also supported.

But in the same poem the Jesuit wrote:

> What makes the man and what
> The man within that makes:
> Ask whom he serves or not
> Serves and what side he takes.
>
> For good grows wild and wide,
> Has shades, is nowhere none;
> But right must seek a side,
> And choose for chieftain one.

In these lines he is concerned not with the work of art as such, but with the artist; not with the end of art, but with the end of man; not with art but with prudence.

While art concerns a local end, says St. Thomas, prudence concerns the whole of human life and its last end. Thus while "the sole end of art is the work itself and its beauty . . . for the man making, the work to be done comes into the line of morality and so is merely a means". The end of the work of art is beauty but the end of man is God. "If the artist", according to this view "were to take for the final end of his activity, that is to say, for beatitude, the end of his art or the beauty of his work, he would be, purely and simply, an idolater".

All poets may be—and ultimately must be—judged from both points of view. The great devotional poet must be at the same time a great poet and a deeply religious man.

---

* Prudence, in this context, or "practical wisdom", means a comprehensive purpose of good: in spite of misleading language, it does not necessarily connote "enlightened self-interest".

The Wreck of the Deutschland

THE story of how the poet broke his silence in 1875 and wrote "The Wreck of the Deutschland" is best told in his own words in a famous letter to Dixon:

> What I had written I burnt before I became a Jesuit and re-solved to write no more, as not belonging to my profession, unless it were by the wish of my superiors; so for seven years I wrote nothing but two or three little presentation pieces which occasion called for. But when in the winter of '75 the Deutschland was wrecked in the mouth of the Thames and five Franciscan nuns, exiles from Germany by the Falck Laws [a part of Bismarck's Kulturkampf], aboard of her were drowned, I was affected by the account and, happening to say so to my rector, he said that he wished someone would write a poem on the subject. On this hint I set to work, and though my hand was out at first, produced one. I had long had haunting my ear the echo of a new rhythm which I now realized on paper.[1]

While seven years of poetical silence lay behind the poem, seven years of theological studies, religious meditation, and the whole experience of the most formative period of a Jesuit's life also lay behind it.

But during this period he had not entirely neglected the study of poetry. For a year he had taught "rhetoric" at Manresa House (1873–4) and had pondered the problems of prosody, so that haunting his ear had been a new rhythm which was now to burst out in the urgency and intensity of a poetry different from any he had ever attempted.

But haunting him, too, was a new perception of reality, of a universe which had taken on meaning and significance. And this new vision of the world was to find an opportunity for expression in conjunction with an utterly new way of saying things. "The Wreck of the Deutschland" is far more than a presentation piece in honour of five Franciscan nuns; rather the word of his rector enabled him to tell his own story in telling of their story.

"To read this", says the editor of his letters, "brings to mind pent-up flood waters at last released by the bursting of a dam." And indeed all the immediacy and intensity of seven years of religious life become articulate in this great ode born of silence.

Here is the fullness of the praise, reverence, and service of God which had become his way of life. Here is the very epitome of the Spiritual Exercises in the completeness of the poet's dedication to the imitation of Christ, to the pursuit of the highest ideal, the *alter Christus*. Here was answered the prayer he made when in the Exercises he asked "for an interior knowledge of our Lord, Who for me was made Man, in order that I may love Him better and follow Him more closely"

"*Ipse*, the only one, Christ"—thus the poet tersely sums up the meaning of "The Wreck of the Deutschland". For its meaning is Christ: it is the story of the Passion and Redemption working themselves out in the lives of men; it tells how Christ, "the martyr-master", calls the souls of men to Him, calls them through suffering and sacrifice, through the Cross, to perfection, to Himself—how He appeals to them through the beauty of the world —how submission to Christ is the only true deliverance—how Christ's majesty and terror and might are merely His love trying to bring men "to hero of Calvary, Christ's feet" And the poem narrates the story of a nun and of a poet, Gerard Manley Hopkins, who read in the temporal events surrounding them an eternal message from their God. So completely does it affirm the Way of the Cross that it is no wonder that the poet cries out, "here the faithful waver, the faithless fable and miss"

Analysis cannot exhaust its possibilities, and Bernard Kelly's advice, "Meditate first for a fortnight on the Passion of our Lord", is the soundest admonition any reader can have. But the implications of the ode are so vast and so terribly true that most "waver" before this vision of the meaning of the world.

The poem is genuinely difficult, as Hopkins admitted to Bridges. But most of the difficulty is caused by the fact that so few of us are really Christians and that it is not until the twenty-eighth stanza that something of the meaning bursts upon us in the apocalyptic vision of the nun: *Ipse*.

The ode opens with great sureness of rhythm; the poet has felt the power of God, infinite Master of the world and of men, Who has again asserted Himself and made Himself known:

> Thou mastering me
> God! giver of breath and bread,
> World's strand, sway of the sea;
> Lord of living and dead;

Thou hast bound bones and veins in me, fastened me flesh,
  And after it almost unmade, what with dread,
      Thy doing: and dost thou touch me afresh?
  Over again I feel thy finger and find thee.

But the vast disparity between God and man is already softened in the last lines of this first stanza, where he recognizes that God has raised him by divine grace to a vital act in Christ; for in his Commentary on the Spiritual Exercises he wrote that grace "lifts the receiver from one cleave of being to another and to a vital act in Christ: this is truly God's finger touching the very vein of personality, which nothing else can reach".[2] Thus in a manner he becomes Christ, and Paul and Austin and the nun are all participating in the life of Christ and re-enacting the sacrifice on the Cross.

The next stanza makes it plain that grace does not destroy human nature, but that the will must acquiesce, must co-operate, must say yea to the call from God. And it says emphatically that the struggle of self-abnegation and self-immolation are like a fire passing through us:

        I did say yes
     O at lightning and lashed rod;
  Thou heardst me truer than tongue confess
     Thy terror, O Christ, O God;
Thou knowest the walls, altar and hour and night:
The swoon of a heart that the sweep and the hurl of thee trod
     Hard down with a horror of height:
And the midriff astrain with leaning of, laced with fire of stress.

This I take to be not merely an affirmation that the poet submitted, said yes to the Passion and Redemption working themselves out in the case of the Franciscan nuns, but that in his own personal life he had heard God calling to him from the Cross. What happened to the nun on the deck was foreshadowed in some earlier spiritual crisis in the life of Hopkins, most likely when he first experienced the full impact of the Spiritual Exercises and felt God's finger upon him, but only "Thou knowest the walls, altar and hour and night". Here, as well as throughout the poem, it is well to recall Hopkins' words to the incredulous Bridges: "What refers to myself in the poem is all strictly and literally true and did all occur; nothing is added for poetical padding."[3]

St. Ignatius' "Two Standards" are powerfully suggested in the next lines; here we have the bold audacity of the saint of God who surrenders to be delivered, who dies to live:

> The frown of his face
> Before me, the hurtle of hell
> Behind, where, where was a, where was a place?
> I whirled out wings that spell
> And fled with a fling of the heart to the heart of the Host.
> My heart, but you were dovewinged, I can tell,
> Carrier-witted, I am bold to boast,
> To flash from the flame to the flame then, tower from the grace to the grace.

Indeed these stanzas suggest his experiences with the sections of the Exercises leading up to the "Election", when after wrestling with God he surrendered himself into His Hands, fled to the "heart of the Host" and answered the call to be a son of Ignatius, to welcome the life of Christ.

After the hurtle of the first three stanzas comes this, which restrainedly recognizes that only grace makes possible this submission; that it is the natural life which disintegrates, while the supernatural life, the life of grace, is the only source of strength:

> I am soft sift
> In an hourglass—at the wall
> Fast, but mined with a motion, a drift,
> And it crowds and it combs to the fall;
> I steady as a water in a well, to a poise, to a pane,
> But roped with, always, all the way down from the tall
> Fells or flanks of the voel, a vein
> Of the gospel proffer, a pressure, a principle, Christ's gift.*

And "Christ's gift", redemptive grace, which he will soon refer to as the divine "stress", is, he tells us in his Commentary on the Spiritual Exercises,

> Any action, activity, on God's part by which, in creating or after creating, he carries the creature to or towards the end of its being, which is its self-sacrifice to God and its salvation. It is, I say, any such activity on God's part; so that so far as this action or activity is God's it is divine stress, holy spirit, and, as all is done through Christ, Christ's spirit.[4]

---

* The contrast involves on the one hand the image of human life as the sand in an hourglass as it slowly but steadily disappears and, on the other, of human life as a well, stable and constant, fed by ("roped with") the streams of the mountain ("voel").

Now, he turns in ecstasy to anticipate what is to come: the story how with the aid of this grace all things summon man, especially "the heart, hard at bay", to Christ. Even the beauty of the physical world communicates a message of love calling man to God. But this is true only for the heart which has been illumined by the "instress" of Christ's grace:

> I kiss my hand
> To the stars, lovely-asunder
> Starlight, wafting him out of it; and
> Glow, glory in thunder,
> Kiss my hand to the dappled-with-damson west:
> Since, tho' he is under the world's splendour and wonder,
> His mystery must be instressed, stressed;†
> For I greet him the days I meet him, and bless when I understand.

This mystery stems from the Incarnation, the result of God's assumption of human form, His own immersion, concretely and really, into the actual realm of finite existence. This is the ultimate inexplicable, God-Man. But the Incarnation is also the ultimate proof of the indwelling of the Divine in the natural. The call of Christ in the beauty of the world, inviting man to his own redemption and salvation, stems, then, from the graces of Christ's suffering and passion. And the next stanza develops this very profound theme. No wonder that Coventry Patmore said, "The one secret, the greatest of all, is the Doctrine of the Incarnation, regarded not as an historical event which occurred two thousand years ago, but as an event which is renewed in the body of every one who is in the way to the fulfilment of his original destiny". And Hopkins wrote to one of his friends: "I think the trivialness of life is, and personally to each one, ought to be seen to be, done away with by the Incarnation."[5]

The above is what I have called Hopkins' "new vision" of the world which opened before him as his religious life deepened and as he lived the Spiritual Exercises. Even the physical world took on a completely new significance. "Suppose", he wrote in commenting on "The Contemplation to Obtain Love", "God showed us in a vision the whole world enclosed first in a drop of water, allowing everything to be seen in its native colours; then the same in a drop of Christ's blood, by which everything whatever

---

† Ordinarily Hopkins uses "instress" verbally and "stress" substantively; here, however, the first is an intensive form of the second, and the impact is heightened by the reversal of the expected word order.

was turned to scarlet, keeping nevertheless mounted in the scarlet its own colour too"—and the second of these worlds is the one he saw as no other poet had ever seen it.[6]

Not out of Christ's heavenly life, "not out of his bliss", springs redemptive grace, the "stress" which "stars and storms deliver" (for the Redemption was the loving sacrifice of Christ in answer to the stroke that man, in the person of Adam, dealt). Not out of "his bliss" came that invitation to the Cross which now "rides time like riding a river" and which makes even "the faithful waver, the faithless fable and miss', as they see the call to the Cross:

> Not out of his bliss
> Springs the stress felt
> Nor first from heaven (and few know this)
> Swings the stroke dealt—
> Stroke and a stress that stars and storms deliver,
> That guilt is hushed by, hearts are flushed by and melt—
> But it rides time like riding a river
> (And here the faithful waver, the faithless fable and miss).

The next stanzas have an unexpressed emphatic "but" standing before them, telling how redemptive grace *does* "spring" from Christ's Incarnation and Passion. "To offer sacrifice was the chief purpose of his life and that the sacrifice of his life", said Hopkins in an unpublished sermon;[7] and the grace He sends to men is the grace to imitate Him:

> It dates from day
> Of his going in Galilee;
> Warm-laid grave of a womb-life grey;
> Manger, maiden's knee;
> The dense and the driven Passion, and frightful sweat;
> Thence the discharge of it, there its swelling to be,
> Though felt before, though in high flood yet—
> What none would have known of it, only the heart, being hard at bay,
>
> Is out with it! Oh,
> We lash with the best or worst
> Word last! How a lush-kept plush-capped sloe
> Will, mouthed to flesh-burst,
> Gush!—flush the man, the being with it, sour or sweet,
> Brim, in a flash, full!*—Hither then, last or first,
> To hero of Calvary, Christ's feet—
> Never ask if meaning it, wanting it, warned of it—men go.

* i.e. Brimfull in a flash.

The prayer that follows is full of a realization of the paradoxes of divine love; its bitterness is sweet, its lightning is affection, and the crosses it sends are its greatest mercy.

> Be adored among men,
> God, three-numberèd form;
> Wring thy rebel, dogged in den,
> Man's malice, with wrecking and storm.
> Beyond saying sweet, past telling of tongue,
> Thou art lightning and love, I found it, a winter and warm;
> Father and fondler of heart thou hast wrung:
> Hast thy dark descending and most art merciful then.

And the final stanza of the first section of the poem flows from the one above, asking God to send His grace to all men:

> With an anvil-ding
> And with fire in him forge thy will
> Or rather, rather then, stealing as Spring
> Through him, melt him but master him still:
> Whether at once, as once at a crash Paul,
> Or as Austin, a lingering-out sweet skill,
> Make mercy in all of us, out of us all
> Mastery, but be adored, but be adored King.

The Second Part of "The Wreck of the Deutschland" tells the story how a Franciscan nun read in the world about her the message of Christ calling her to the Cross. She was one of five,

> Loathed for a love men knew in them,
> Banned by the land of their birth.

In the midst of the trial and suffering, of exile and shipwreck— a story told with great power and even greater beauty—

> . . . a lioness arose breasting the babble,
> A prophetess towered in the tumult, a virginal tongue told.

This seer

> Has one fetch* in her: she rears herself to divine Ears. . . .

In heaven above Christ was waiting, waiting for her to respond to His grace, to flee to Him, "to the heart of the Host", to recognize in this trial a message for her to come to Him. In His sight

---

* Dialect word meaning a deep painful breath or inspiration.

suffering assumed for the sins of the world, for persecution's sake, was beauty:

> Surf, snow, river and earth
> Gnashed: but thou art above, thou Orion of light;
> Thy unchancelling poising palms were weighing the worth,
> Thou martyr-master: in thy sight
> Storm flakes were scroll-leaved flowers, lily showers—sweet heaven
> was astrew in them.

Suffering Christ sees as the special badge of His love, a badge of those who have chosen to imitate Him, of those who wish to be identified with Him, of those who are His chosen ones—for they are being Himself, they are re-enacting the Redemption. Now the poet exclaims at the resemblance between the five nuns and the wounds of the God-Man:

> Five! the finding and sake*
> And cipher of suffering Christ.
> Mark, the mark is of man's make
> And the word of it Sacrificed.
> But he scores it in scarlet himself on his own bespoken,
> Before-time-taken, dearest prizèd and priced—
> Stigma, signal, cinquefoil† token
> For lettering of the lamb's fleece, ruddying of the rose-flake.

And logically we think of St. Francis who bore on his body the marks of the suffering the world had imposed on Christ, and of St. Francis' joy in being able to show his love for Christ in bearing the stigmata:

> Joy fall to thee, father Francis,
> Drawn to the Life that died;
> With the gnarls of the nails in thee, niche of the lance, his
> Lovescape crucified‡

* We might say "index and sign". Hopkins explains the word *sake* as he uses it in another poem: "It is the *sake* of 'for the sake of', *forsake, namesake, keepsake*. I mean by it the being a thing has outside itself, as a voice by its echo, a face by its reflection, a body by its shadow, a man by his name, fame, or memory, *and also* that in the thing by virtue of which especially it has this being abroad, and that is something distinctive, marked, specifically or individually speaking, as for a voice and echo clearness; for a reflected image light, brightness: for a shadow-casting body bulk; for a man genius, great achievements, amiability, and so on." *Letters to Bridges*, p. 83.

† The five-leaved plant or figure.

‡ i.e. Love-in-its-essence here is crucified.

And seal of his seraph-arrival! and these thy daughters
And five-livèd and leavèd favour and pride,
  Are sisterly sealed in wild waters,
To bathe in his fall-gold mercies, to breathe in his all-fire glances.

These two stanzas interrupt the drama being enacted on the deck of the ship, and offer some relief from the intensity of the narration. Back on the ship, the nun is welcoming the Cross and calling to Christ with a cry of loving impatience:

Was calling "O Christ, Christ, come quickly":
The cross to her she calls Christ to her, christens her wild-worst Best.

Then come lines analysing her motives:

The majesty! what did she mean?
Breathe, arch and original Breath.
Is it love in her of the being as her lover had been?
Breathe, body of lovely Death.
They were else-minded then, altogether, the men
Woke thee with a *we are perishing* in the weather of Gennesareth.
  Or is it that she cried for the crown then,
The keener to come at the comfort for feeling the combating keen?

For how to the heart's cheering
The down-dugged ground-hugged grey
Hovers off, the jay-blue heavens appearing
Of pied and peeled May!
Blue-beating and hoary-glow height; or night, still higher,
With belled fire and the moth-soft Milky Way,
  What by your measure is the heaven of desire,
The treasure never eyesight got, nor was ever guessed what for the hearing?

But it was not safety, or comfort, or ease, or reward, or relief that she prayed for when she embraced the Cross:

No, but it was not these.
The jading and jar of the cart,
Time's tasking, it is fathers that asking for ease
Of the sodden-with-its-sorrowing heart,
Not danger, electrical horror; then further it finds
The appealing of the Passion is tenderer in prayer apart:
  Other, I gather, in measure her mind's
Burden, in wind's burly and beat of endragonèd seas.

"These meanings, that a mind less pitilessly direct would have rested in", Bernard Kelly has admirably said, "the poet sweeps aside. They are the half-way houses, the less perfect. Relentlessly he strips them off from the naked, the stark perfection of the act which follows; and his mind staggers at the coming of it." Here is the climax of the great ode, the point at which the meaning of the whole, the First as well as the Second Part, explodes upon one with a force beyond the bounds of mere vocabulary:

> But how shall I . . . make me room there:
> Reach me a . . . Fancy, come faster—
> Strike you the sight of it? look at it loom there,
> Thing that she . . . there then! the Master,
> *Ipse*, the only one, Christ, King, Head.

Here is the perfect oblation, the perfect self-sacrifice, the perfect self-fulfilment, the Christus and the *alter Christus*.

And now the poem necessarily goes into a diminuendo, and anything that follows must be an anti-climax.

But the next stanza reinforces our interpretation of the whole poem:

> Ah! there was a heart right!
> There was single eye!
> Read the unshapeable shock night
> And knew the who and the why;
> Wording it how but by him that present and past,
> Heaven and earth are word of, worded by?—
> The Simon Peter of a soul! to the blast
> Tarpeian-fast, but a blown beacon of light.

"To whom else shall we go, Lord?" Hopkins, later in his life, writing his Commentary on the Spiritual Exercises and trying to express in prose the meaning of the world and of man's life, stated in almost syllogistic form what he said in this stanza and throughout the ode:

> God's utterance of himself in himself is God the Word, outside himself is this world. This world then is word, expression, news, of God. Therefore its end, its purpose, its purport, its meaning, is God, and its life or work to name and praise him.[8]

In the world, then, man may read the message of the Word, of the Incarnation, of the Redeemer. And what is the greatest praise that man can give? To re-enact the Incarnation and Redemption, to be Christ. Thus the Jesuit added to the above passage, "The

world, man, should after its own manner give God being in return
for that being he has given. This is done by the great sacrifice.
To contribute then to that sacrifice is the end for which man was
made".[9]

And the poem ends with a series of stanzas, prayers, increasing
in the fullness and majesty and grandeur of their music to the
very last intercession:

> Dame, at our door
> Drowned, and among our shoals,
> Remember us in the roads, the heaven-haven of the Reward:
> Our King back,* oh, upon English souls!
> Let him easter in us, be a dayspring to the dimness of us, be a
> crimson-cresseted east,
> More brightening her, rare-dear Britain, as his reign rolls,
> Pride, rose, prince, hero of us, high-priest,
> Our hearts' charity's hearth's fire, our thoughts' chivalry's throng's
> Lord.

Such, then, was the vision of the world which Hopkins saw
through "a drop of Christ's blood, by which everything whatever
was turned to scarlet, keeping nevertheless mounted in the
scarlet its own colour too".

Like some great landmark, "The Wreck of the Deutschland"
cleaves sharply between two very definite periods of Hopkins'
work, between his early verse and his great poetry, between
Oxford and the Society of Jesus. And this new and great poetry
differs from the earlier poetry in far more than mere metrical
resources and technical richness. The advance in thought is even
greater. The examination of one of his Oxford poems makes this
immediately clear. In "Nondum" there is no perception of any
relationship between God and nature, and the result is that there
is no relationship between God and man. That poem opens with
an address to the vast silence:

> God, though to Thee our psalm we raise
> No answering voice comes from the skies;
> To Thee the trembling sinner prays
> But no forgiving voice replies;
> Our prayer seems lost in desert ways,
> Our hymn in the vast silence dies.

The poet was aware of the awful glory of all the earth and nature,
more awful still because he could find no real sign of God:

* May (our King) be back.

> We see the glories of the earth
> But not the hand that wrought them all:
> Night to a myriad worlds gives birth,
> Yet like a lighted empty hall
> Where stands no host at door or hearth
> Vacant creation's lamps appal.

Such an attitude had very naturally resulted in a pseudo-mysticism or pseudo-asceticism in which the young Hopkins tried to cast off his body, to live only in the spirit: "Be shellèd, eyes". This results in that puritanism (that false substitute for genuine asceticism) which is really manichean in its implications. Now whether the young Hopkins was indulging in this heretical view of man or whether he was starting on the purgative path of a true asceticism, which for a time severely disciplines the senses so that they may be purified and fully realized, is really unimportant. The important thing is that he did advance to a new vision of the world and of man in which he saw "God in all things and all things in God", and in which the physical universe became "word, expression, news of God".

The sacramentalism of Scotus and the Spiritual Exercises, the realization of the far-reaching implications of the Incarnation, the full dedication of all the powers of man to the "praise, reverence, and service of God" give his mature poems their combination of sensitivity to created beauty—a vital awareness even more appealing than his earlier Keatsian sensuousness—and their intellectual and emotional direction. "Such divination of the spiritual in the things of sense, which also will express itself in the things of sense", Maritain has penetratingly remarked, "is what we properly call poetry".

The qualities of his new poetry sprang from his reintegrated character, from his realization that he himself ("Thou hast bound bones and veins in me, fastened me flesh") was like unto Christ ("the heaven-flung, heart-fleshed"), that indeed his whole *raison d'être* was to go through the world to Christ as Christ had come from the heavens to man.

After we have read this first really great poem of Hopkins, we can well address him with the words of his contemporary, Francis Thompson:

> God has given thee visible thunders
> To utter thine apocalypse of wonders.

Poems: 1877-8

FROM 1875, when he broke his poetic silence, till the end of 1878, Hopkins completed some sixteen poems. What he wrote in 1876 is of little interest; it was as if the composition of "The Wreck of the Deutschland" had drained him of his poetic energy. However, four poems do survive: "Moonrise", a sketch of the early morning, "The Woodlark", a fragment, "Penmaen Pool", ten facile but unpoetic stanzas for the visitors' book at an inn, and "Silver Jubilee". The last, the only religious poem of the group, was written in honour of the Bishop of Shrewsbury's twenty-fifth year of episcopacy; it hardly rises above the level of ordinary occasional verse.

But 1877 was rich in its harvest: ten of his most delightful and exuberant religious poems were written in the months just preceding his ordination (23rd September, 1877) and in those immediately after he had become a Jesuit priest. 1878 added three more poems to his body of religious verse.

These poems of 1877-8, like "The Wreck of the Deutschland", were the fruit of his broken silence, but they have a smoother flow than the ode of 1875. Yet the recurrent motifs of these compositions are implicitly contained in the earlier poem. The same sacramental view of nature is expressed, the same realization that God must win His creatures to Him. The same technical devices, now not so obviously new, are further elaborated and developed.

A religious experience of beauty is the central theme that runs through most of these poems—an experience of created things moulded and directed by the Spiritual Exercises. We must recall once more—for its echo is found all through the poems of this period—Hopkins' own succinct statement of the meaning and purpose of all things—his précis of the "Principle and Foundation":

> God's utterance of himself in himself is God the Word, outside himself is this world. This world then is word, expression, news, of God. Therefore its end, its purpose, its purport, its meaning, is God, and its life or work to name and praise Him.

Here is stated that sacramental view of nature which sees all things as avenues to the supreme Being. Man may rise from an experience of particular things, of "inscapes", to God; he may find in the many the One. Natural beauty can bring man to higher Beauty. Indeed did not Scotus contend that the world existed for the very purpose of bridging the gap between finite man and the Infinite?

The poems of 1877-8 show how the world expresses God and praises Him. But Hopkins' growing concern is with man. Does he perceive the world as a constant call to perfection? Does he use created things to pursue his own end which is also God? The contrast between the beauty of created things as a message from God, and man, his blindness and waywardness, give to many of Hopkins' poems their peculiar vitality and beauty.

The poems of these two years are full of joyous wonder at the beauty of the world, of a joy enhanced because creation is seen sacramentally and because he himself is using beauty to praise his Maker. No longer do we find the versifying of unrealized abstractions as in his Oxford poems. Nor are the poems surfeited with the lushness and luxuriance of his "Vision of the Mermaids". The senses are not suppressed, but they are directed. They become instruments and means with which to praise God. There is an integration of sense, intellect, and emotion in one act in rhythm of sound and colour, this curtal sonnet sees in the variety of nature participations in God; but not until the last line does the spiritual and material, in one universal pattern of which God is the design.

The joy in the variegated and transient "inscapes" of the world is Franciscan in its eagerness in "Pied Beauty". A wimpling rhythm of sound and colour, this curtal-sonnet sees in the variety of nature participations in God; but not until the last lines does the poet pull all together and touch the spark which gives the whole its direction and aim:

> Glory be to God for dappled* things—
>   For skies of couple-colour as a brinded† cow;
>   For rose-moles all in stipple upon trout that swim;
> Fresh-firecoal chestnut-falls; finches' wings;
>   Landscape plotted and pieced—fold, fallow, and plough;
>   And áll trádes, their gear and tackle and trim.

---

* Variegated, pied.   † Pied, spotted.

All things counter, original, spare, strange;
    Whatever is fickle, freckled (who knows how?)
      With swift, slow; sweet, sour; adazzle, dim;
He fathers-forth whose beauty is past change:
        Praise him.

In the last line all the preceding Scotist "inscapes" raise the poet to "Immutable Beauty" They have particularized beauty, but God is Beauty in Itself. Yet it is by knowing transient beauty, the many, that the heart mounts up to the unchanging One. Hopkins shares the Pauline vision: "For the invisible things of Him, from the creation of the world, are clearly seen, being understood by the things that are made." St. Thomas had emphasized that "as all the perfections of creatures descend in order from God, who is the highest of perfection, man should begin from the lower creatures and ascend by degrees, and so advance to the knowledge of God". And St. Bonaventure had pointed out the same road: "The creatures of this visible world signify the invisible attributes of God, because God is the source, model and last end of every creature, and because every effect points to its cause, every image to its model, every road to its goal."

The "inscapes" which Hopkins poured into "Pied Beauty", itself an "inscape" of delicate variety and pattern, lifted him to a higher and more exalted Beauty—but the sacramental world remained to be enjoyed, yet not to be worshipped as Beauty Absolute. Yet this is a thing that is often misunderstood. Plato himself had said that "the true order of going . . . is to use the beauties of earth as steps along which he mounts upwards for the sake of that other Beauty" But the whole Platonist tradition tended to despise created beauty for the sake of Uncreated Beauty. The Christian tradition was essentially different, in spite of the frequent "contempt of creatures" which one finds; for, as Maritain has written,

> This phrase, which primarily exhibits the weakness of human language, must not be misunderstood. The saint sees in practical fact the nothingness of creatures with regard to the Being he loves and the End he has chosen. It is a loving contempt of all things other than that beloved. And the more he despises creatures in the degree to which they might be rivals of God, or objects of a possible choice to the exclusion of God, the more he cherishes them as loved by God, and made by Him as fair and worthy of our love. . . . So we understand the paradox whereby in the end the saint includes

in a universal love of kinship and of piety—incomparably more free, but also more tender and more happy, than any selfish love of the voluptuary or the miser—all the weakness and the beauty of things, all he had left behind him on his journey.

And in the very Constitutions of his Order Hopkins was taught to place his affection in the Creator of all things, "loving Him in all creatures and them all in Him, according to His most holy and divine Will". (Rule 17)

True, in these poems there is greater intensity than in Walt Whitman, that poet so like and yet so unlike Hopkins. Yet it is a misunderstanding of a religious position to speak, as does Robert Bridges, of "the naked encounter of sensualism and asceticism" in the poetry of Hopkins. The critics of the Jesuit have gone very wide of the mark in their failure to understand the attitude behind these poems. Frances Winwar has written that "something which he could not altogether confine to Christian purpose betrayed itself in his work, containing more of Pater's concentration of feeling in a single verse than Wilde's whole volume". Herbert Read has said that such a poem as "The Windhover" is completely objective in its senseful catalogue, but that Hopkins got over his scruples by declaring the poem "To Christ our Lord". And very recently Philip Henderson has contended that in spite of himself Hopkins' appreciation of nature was dangerously pagan.

All these critics are amazed to find a Jesuit who can communicate the loveliness of God's world with such haunting appreciation. They, rather than Hopkins, may be said to be the victims of that puritanism which Monsignor Ronald Knox refers to as the Englishman's substitute for asceticism.

"Pied Beauty" and the other poems of this group—indeed all that Hopkins ever wrote—are the poet's *Laudate Dominum* in which he calls on all creation to praise their Creator; for, as Peter the Venerable said, when the world ceases to offer sacrifice to God, it will cease to be God's. The secret behind these poems is expressed tersely in two lines from "Ash-Boughs":

> It is old earth's groping towards the steep
> Heaven whom she childs us by

Thus another priest has recently reminded us: 'Art has as its ultimate object the playing of a priestly role, to sanctify nature, and lead it back to God. The Christian artist gives to silent creation a voice and the wherewithal to satisfy its deepest desire: praise."

And those who still doubt that the Christian may look on creation as did its Creator, seeing all things as good, that he may see the world without falling into either pantheistic tremors or Manichean hate, might well ponder Chesterton's words as St. Francis, reborn, looked upon a new world:

> The flower and stars have recovered their first innocence, fire and water are felt to be worthy to be the brother and sister of a saint. The purge of paganism is complete at last.
>
> For water itself has been washed. Fire itself has been purified as by fire. Water is no longer that water into which slaves were flung to feed the fishes. Fire is no longer that fire through which children were passed to Moloch. Flowers smell no more of the forgotten garlands gathered in the garden of Priapus; stars stand no more as signs of the far frigidity of gods as cold as those cold fires. They are all like things newly made and awaiting new names, from one who shall come to name them. Neither the universe nor the earth have now any longer the old sinister significance of the world. They await a new reconciliation with man, but they are already capable of being reconciled Man has stripped from his soul the last rag of nature-worship, and can return to nature.

Thus it is that a Jesuit like Hopkins can be at the same time a priest true to heaven and a poet true to earth.

More delicately fanciful than "Pied Beauty" is "The Starlight Night", in which the beauty about him is conceived as the outer wall of heaven, a midpoint at which the world touches the periphery of Beauty, Christ. In the octet, the mind in white heat captures the "inscapes" of the sky in a series of exclamatory images:

> Look at the stars! look, look up at the skies!
>   O look at all the fire-folk sitting in the air!
>   The bright boroughs, the circle-citadels there!
> Down in dim woods the diamond delves!* the elves'-eyes!
> The grey lawns cold where gold, where quickgold lies!
>   Wind-beat whitebeam!† airy abeles‡ set on a flare!
>   Flake-doves sent floating forth at a farmyard scare!—
> Ah well! it is all a purchase, all is a prize.

* i.e. dens, pits.
  † The small tree, *Pyrus Aria*, having large leaves with white silky hairs on the under sides.
  ‡ White poplars.

The last line has made the theme explicit: by a disciplined and directed use of created beauty all may rise to Beauty even higher. The sestet continues:

> Buy then! bid then!—What?—Prayer, patience, alms, vows.
> Look, look: a May-mess, like on orchard boughs!
>   Look! March-bloom, like on mealed-with-yellow sallows!*
> These are indeed the barn; withindoors house
> The shocks. This piece-bright paling shuts the spouse
>   Christ home, Christ and his mother and all his hallows.

One is inevitably reminded of an experience Hopkins had recorded in his Journal, where he told how one August evening in 1874 "as we drove home the stars came out thick: I leant back to look at them and my heart opening more than usual praised our Lord to and in whom all that beauty comes home". His Ignatian training had indeed opened his heart very wide when he came to write such poems as "The Starlight Night".

In "The May Magnificat" the tremulous beauty of Spring symbolizes the purity and beauty of Mary. The poem abounds with joy in the appeal of the growing world.

> When drop-of-blood-and-foam-dapple
> Bloom lights the orchard-apple
>   And thicket and thorp† are merry
>   With silver-surfèd‡ cherry
>
> And azuring-over greybell makes
> Wood banks and brakes§ wash wet like lakes
>   And magic cuckoocall
>   Caps, clears, and clinches all.

But the lines are not merely a collection of attractive sensuous images, of "inscapes" flung together in verse form. Rather, all the senses are employed as instruments to praise Mary:

> This ecstasy all through mothering earth
> Tells Mary her mirth till Christ's birth
>   To remember and exultation
>   In God who was her salvation.

The whole poem was written as an occasional piece to be hung,

---

* Willows.
† Hamlet, village.
‡ Surfaced with silver, or foamed with silver-white.
§ Thickets.

anonymously, before the Lady Statue at Stonyhurst during May, when it was the custom to compose verses to Mary. Obviously it is not in his characteristic manner, for it was an attempt to appeal to the popular taste and Hopkins admitted that in such writing he usually felt himself "to come short". But I see no indication that Hopkins was dissatisfied for the reason that, as Claude Colleer Abbott suggests, "the lush, yet fresh, beauty of the descriptive writing, which conveys the very 'feel' of May-time, clashes inevitably with praise of the Virgin Mary". That is utterly to misunderstand the function of the senses and of created beauty.

But the poem of this group that is born of his greatest exuberance, bringing to an emotional crescendo his experience of beauty, is "Hurrahing in Harvest". It bears the stamp of an almost ecstatic experience of the sacramental operation of nature upon him. Indeed Hopkins himself told Bridges that it was "the outcome of half an hour of extreme enthusiasm as I walked home alone one day from fishing in the Elwy".[1] Three years later he was attempting to express in another art form that memorable half hour's "spontaneous overflow of powerful feeling", for he was trying to set the piece to music.

The poem opens with his declaration of the "inscapes" he had experienced in lines charged with joyous wonder at the beauty of created things:

> Summer ends now; now, barbarous in beauty, the stooks* arise
> Around; up above, what wind-walks! what lovely behaviour
> Of silk-sack clouds! has wilder, wilful-wavier
> Meal-drift moulded ever and melted across skies?

But the lines that follow have even greater vigour and delight—a delight born of rare spiritual joy. Confronted with created beauty, the heart flushed with it experiences it as news of God:

> I walk, I lift up, I lift up heart, eyes,
> Down all that glory in the heavens to glean our Saviour;
> And, èyes, heárt, what looks, what lips yet gave you a
> Rapturous love's greeting of realer, of rounder replies?

Here is an experimental "instress" of a "rapturous love's greeting"—an infusion of the being with beauty and its message of divine love. It is testimony that Hopkins' arduous practice of the

---

* Dialect word for stocks of corn.

Spiritual Exercises culminated in the final "Contemplation to Obtain Love".

The next lines firmly and powerfully praise God as the very "ground of being, and granite of it":

> And the azurous hung hills are his world-wielding shoulder
>   Majestic—as a stallion stalwart, very-violet-sweet!*

Then comes the consummation in ecstatic desire for union:

> These things, these things were here and but the beholder
>   Wanting; which two when they once meet,
> The heart rears wings bold and bolder
>   And hurls for him, O half hurls earth for him off under his feet.

Such a climax, an experience of earthly beauty as powerfully pulling man to God and of man co-operating by rapturously flying to Divine Love, is analogous to the religious experience of "The Wreck of the Deutschland". Even some of the imagery is the same:

>   I whirled out wings that spell
> And fled with a fling of the heart to the heart of the Host.
> My heart, but you were dovewinged, I can tell,
>   Carrier-witted, I am bold to boast,
> To flash from the flame to the flame then, tower from the grace to the
>   grace.

And again he reads aright the message in the world:

> Wording it how but by him that present and past,
> Heaven and earth are word of, worded by?

The whole tradition of Catholic thought was a force in moulding such an attitude. St. Augustine had written:

> Thy whole creation ceaseth not, nor is silent in Thy praise: neither the spirit of man directed unto Thee, nor creation animate or inanimate, by the voice of those who meditate thereon: that so our souls may from their weariness arise towards Thee, leaning on those things which Thou hast created, and passing on to Thyself, who madest them wonderfully; and there is refreshment and true strength.

The Directory had urged every Jesuit to ponder carefully such

---

* The image has been explained by Laura Riding and Robert Graves as "a phrase reconciling the two seemingly opposed qualities of mountains, their male, animal-like roughness and strength and at the same time their ethereal quality under soft light. . . ."

passages in St. Augustine's Confessions, and we know that Hopkins was devoted to the great Bishop of Hippo.

But throughout it was especially the Spiritual Exercises which were the primary force behind his poems. This is very clearly seen if we examine the notes that Hopkins wrote for an address based on the "Principle and Foundation". We do not know the date of these jottings, nor do we know their occasion. But we do know that they parallel closely—even to very phrases—the poems of 1877-8. And they reinforce, once more, our testimony of the extent to which Hopkins' new vision sprang from his spiritual life as a Jesuit.

These notes consider first the meaning of creation and its end; then Hopkins asks: do created things fulfil their purpose? Especially does man?

With an abundance of homely figures—some of the most delightful prose Hopkins ever wrote—the address unfolds the implications of St. Ignatius' teaching:

> Why did God create? . . . He meant the world to give him praise, reverence, and service; *to give him glory.* It is like a garden, a field he sows: what should it bear him? praise, reverence, and service; it should yield him glory. It is an estate he farms: what should it bring him in? Praise, reverence and service; it should repay him glory. It is a leasehold he lets out: what should its rent be? Praise, reverence, and service; its rent is his glory. It is a bird he teaches to sing, a pipe, a harp he plays on: what should it sing to him? etc. It is a glass he looks in: what should it shew him? With praise, reverence, and service it should shew him his own glory. It is a book he has written, of the riches of his knowledge, teaching endless truths, full lessons of wisdom, a poem of beauty: what is it about? His praise, the reverence due to him, the way to serve him; it tells him of his glory. It is a censer fuming: what is the sweet incense? His praise, his reverence, his service; it rises to his glory. It is an altar and a victim lying in his sight: why is it offered? To his praise, honour, and service: it is a sacrifice to his glory.

In the next section Hopkins looks about him at created things, exclusive of man, to see whether they fulfil this purpose of expressing and praising God; his answer is:

> The sun and stars shining glorify God. They stand where he placed them, they move where he bid them. "The heavens declare the glory of God."

Then come important distinctions and qualifications:

> They glorify God, *but they do not know it*. The birds sing to him,
> the thunder speaks of his terror, the lion is like his strength, the
> sea is like his greatness, the honey like his sweetness; they are
> something like him, they make him known, they tell of him, they
> give him glory, but they do not know they do, they do not know
> him. . . . This then is poor praise, faint reverence, slight service,
> dull glory. Nevertheless what they can *they always do*.

Pied and dappled things, "lovely-asunder starlight", "the
dappled-with-damson west", "skies of couple-colour", "March-
bloom", May-time's "drop-of-blood-and-foam-dapple", the
"silk-sack clouds"—all these created things are news of God and
praise Him though they do not know they do. Yet only through
man is their beauty really sacramental.

Then Hopkins turns to consider man whom he calls "life's
pride and cared-for-crown" in the hierarchy of beings. St.
Thomas had called him the noblest thing in nature and the Psalmist
put him just after the angels. If man uses nature sacramentally
he is fulfilling his purpose; if he employs created beauty to raise
him to Beauty he is pursuing his end.

> But amidst them all is man, man and the angels: we will speak of
> man. Man was created. Like the rest then to praise, reverence,
> and serve God; to give him glory. He does so, even by his being,
> beyond all visible creatures: "What a piece of work is man!"
> (Expand by "Domine, Dominus, quam admirabile, etc. . . . Quid
> est homo. . . . Minuisti eum paulo minus ab angelis.") But man
> can know God, *can mean to give him glory*. This then was why he
> was made, to give God glory and to mean to give it; to praise God
> freely, willingly to reverence him, gladly to serve him. Man was
> made to give, and mean to give, God glory.

Then he asks whether man actually does pursue his end and
purpose and give God glory. Again the images pour forth in
abundant variation upon the same theme:

> Does man then do it? Never mind others now nor the race of
> man: Do I do it?—If I sin I do not: how can I dishonour God and
> honour him? wilfully dishonour him and yet be meaning to honour
> him? . . . No, we have not answered God's purpose, we have not
> reached the end of our being. Are we God's orchard or God's
> vineyard? we have yielded rotten fruit, sour grapes, or none. Are
> we his cornfield sown? we have not come to ear or are mildewed

in the ear. Are we his farm? it is a losing one to him. Are we his tenants? we have refused him rent. Are we his singing bird? we will not learn to sing. Are we his pipe or harp? we are out of tune, we grate upon his ear. Are we his glass to look in? we are deep in dust or our silver gone or we are broken or, worst of all, we misshape his face and make God's image hideous. Are we his book? we are blotted, we are scribbled over with foulness and blasphemy. Are we his censer? we breathe stench and not sweetness. Are we his sacrifice? we are like the sacrifice of Balac, or Core, and of Cain. If we have sinned we are all this.[2]

The contrast expressed in these notes between nature as instinctively and automatically yet unconsciously praising or expressing God and man as wayward and sinful, failing to use nature sacramentally—this contrast becomes the hinge on which several of the 1877-8 poems turn.

"God's Grandeur" opens with an explosive metaphor expressing the immanence of God. The poet's awareness of created beauty as a reflection of God is so intense that he cannot understand why it is not obvious to all men.

> The world is charged with the grandeur of God.
>   It will flame out, like shining from shook foil;
>   It gathers to a greatness, like the ooze of oil
> Crushed. Why do men then now not reck his rod?

The next quatrain sets in contrast man's use of nature, his failure to recognize it as news and praise and grandeur of God, his failure to use created things to pursue his own end. The lines are also a summary of the particular sins of the nineteenth century:

> Generations have trod, have trod, have trod;
>   And all is seared with trade; bleared, smeared with toil;
>   And wears man's smudge and shares man's smell: the soil
> Is bare now, nor can foot feel, being shod.

Then the sestet rounds out the contrast by stressing the constant renewal and renascence of natural beauty. Why?—because God continues to express Himself in the world:

> And for all this, nature is never spent;
>   There lives the dearest freshness deep down things;
> And though the last lights off the black West went
>   Oh, morning, at the brown brink eastward, springs—
> Because the Holy Ghost over the bent
>   World broods with warm breast and with ah! bright wings.

This last is no mere fanciful image. This recognition of "dearest freshness deep down things" is more than a cold intellectual perception that by his Presence, Essence, and Power, God is in all things. It is an experience, rather, of one flushed by the intuition that the world brings to the sensitive heart, a message loaded with divine love. That this is no mere subjective reading of the poem we can see from a study of Hopkins' notes on the joyful climax to the Spiritual Exercises, the "Contemplation to Obtain Love". There St. Ignatius urges man to look on the created world about him as an effort of God to communicate His love to man, as a vision of God's love. Hopkins' notations in his Commentary are fragmentary, and the thought is theologically difficult. He wrote:

> This contemplation . . . is the contemplation of the Holy Ghost sent to us through creatures. Observe then it is on love and the Holy Ghost is called Love . . . shown "in operibus", the works of God's finger; . . . consisting "in communicatione" etc., and the Holy Ghost as he is the bond and mutual love of Father and Son, so of God and man; that the Holy Ghost is uncreated grace and the sharing by man of the divine nature and the bestowal of himself by God on man.

That Hopkins was experiencing the physical universe as a bond between God and man, as a message from the Divine Goodness, as "news, word, expression" of the Eternal Lover, is further emphasized by three lines he added to the above passage: "All things therefore are charged with love, are charged with God and if we know how to touch them give off sparks and take fire, yield drops and flow, ring and tell of him"[3]—words which have their poetical counterpart in.

> The world is charged with the grandeur of God.
> It will flame out, like shining from shook foil.

In such expressions—as in all sacramentalism—there is the danger of pantheistic language. There are few theologians who have expressed more clearly the immanence and transcendence of God than Hopkins when he wrote in his Commentary:

> God is so deeply present to everything ("Tu autem, O bone omnipotens, eras superior summo meo et interior intimo meo") that it would be impossible for him but for his infinity not to be identified with them or, from the other side, impossible but for his

infinity so to be present to them. This is oddly expressed, I see; I mean—a being so intimately present as God is to other things would be identified with them were it not for God's infinity or were it not for God's infinity he could not be so intimately present to things.[4]

The antithesis between the beauty of nature and man and his use of created things is calmer and less "charged with God" in a poem Hopkins wrote soon after going to Oxford to take up his duties at St. Aloysius' Church in 1878. That he had an affection for the landscape around Oxford is clear from his own undergraduate diary; that his love for it continued is evident in a letter which he wrote to Canon Dixon when he returned there as a Jesuit priest:

> You will see that I have again changed my abode and am returned to my Alma Mater and need not go far to have before my eyes "the little-headed willows two and two" and that landscape, the charm of Oxford, green shouldering grey, which is already abridged and soured and perhaps will soon be put out altogether.[5]

In this prose passage he also indicates his disapproval of nineteenth-century mercantilism which had "seared with trade, bleared, smeared" the beauty which was meant to bring man to God.

The first quatrain of "Duns Scotus's Oxford" captures the charm and appeal of the university town:

> Towery city and branchy between towers;
> Cuckoo-echoing, bell-swarmèd, lark-charmèd, rook-racked,
>   river-rounded;
> The dapple-eared lily below thee; that country and town did
> Once encounter in, here coped and poisèd powers.*

The next lines sketch the effect of man's use of created things— as in "God's Grandeur", except that they are not as direct in their judgment

> Thou hast a base and brickish skirt there,† sours
> That neighbour-nature thy grey beauty is grounded
> Best in; graceless growth, thou hast confounded‡
> Rural rural keeping—folk, flocks, and flowers.

---

* A reference to the time when there was the correct relationship and balance and equipoise between country and town.
† Probably an allusion to the Oxford suburbs.
‡ Confused, ruined, destroyed.

Yet in the sestet of this poem, Hopkins finds some consolation in the beauties which remain, in the memory of the great mediaeval Franciscan who had shown him how to direct his experience of "inscapes" to God:

> Yet ah! this air I gather and I release
> He lived on; these weeds and waters, these walls are what
> He haunted who of all men most sways my spirits to peace;
> Of realty* the rarest-veined unraveller; a not
> Rivalled insight, be rival Italy or Greece;
> Who fired France for Mary without spot.

The contrast between natural beauty, ever renewing its hymn to God, and man, wayward and silent, is far more explicit and direct in "The Sea and the Skylark":

> On ear and ear two noises too old to end
> Trench†—right, the tide that ramps against the shore;
> With a flood or a fall, low lull-off or all roar,
> Frequenting there while moon shall wear and wend.

In vibrant contrast to "the tide that ramps against the shore", comes the exquisitely beautiful image of the song of the skylark as the unskeining of a rolled ribbon swirling and fluttering to the earth:

> Left hand, off land, I hear the lark ascend,
> His rash-fresh‡ re-winded new-skeinèd score
> In crisps of curl off wild winch whirl, and pour
> And pelt music, till none's to spill nor spend.

* Reality.
† i.e. make a trench, groove, furrow.
‡ Explained in a letter: " 'Rash-fresh . . . ' (it is dreadful to explain these things in cold blood) means a headlong and exciting new snatch of singing, resumption by the lark of his song, which by turns he gives over and takes up again all day long, and this goes on, the sonnet says, through all time, without ever losing its first freshness, being a thing both new and old. . . . The skein and coil are the lark's song, which from his height gives the impression (not to me only) of something falling to the earth and not vertically quite but tricklingly or wavingly, something as a skein of silk ribbed by having been tightly wound on a narrow card or a notched holder or as fishing tackle or twine unwinding from a reel or winch: the laps or folds are the notes or short measures and bars of them. The same is called a score in the musical sense of score and this score is 'writ upon a liquid sky trembling to welcome it', only not horizontally. The lark in wild glee races the reel round, paying or dealing out and down the turns of the skein or coil right to the earth floor, the ground, where it lies in a heap, as it were, or rather is all wound off on to another winch, reel, bobbin, or spool in Fancy's eye by the moment the bird touches earth and so is ready for a fresh unwinding at the next flight." *Letters to Bridges*, p. 164.

In opposition to the shimmering beauty of the skylark's song and "the low lull-off or all roar" of the sea is man, created also to sing his hymn of praise, reverence, and service to God. But does he? The entire sestet is devoted to the answer:

> How these two shame this shallow and frail town!
> How ring right out our sordid turbid time,
> Being pure! We, life's pride and cared-for crown,
> Have lost that cheer and charm of earth's past prime:
> Our make and making break, are breaking, down
> To man's last dust, drain fast towards man's first slime.

Our race and civilization are fast draining towards the slime from which we were created—our materialism is leading us literally back to matter instead of raising us through matter to Heaven. We have forgotten our duty to God. "Are we his singing birds?" Hopkins asks in his notes on the "Principle and Foundation"; he shakes his head, "We will not learn to sing".

Thus in several poems of this period, the poet prays that God may send to man the grace that will complete him so that he will be enabled "to give God glory and to mean to give it; to praise God freely, willingly to reverence him, gladly to serve Him".

"In the Valley of the Elwy" (1877) contrasts the beauty of Wales with man who fails to see in this beauty a call to God. The Welsh landscape had attracted Hopkins from the time when as a seminarian he first entered St. Beuno's; it operated on him with a religious impact. "Looking all around but most in looking far up the valley", he entered into his Journal a week after he arrived there in 1874, "I felt an instress and charm of Wales. Indeed in coming here I began to feel a desire to do something for the conversion of Wales". The same desire is in the sonnet he wrote three years later. He referred to Wales as "always to me a mother of Muses".[6] The mother of muses was with him when he wrote "In the Valley of the Elwy":

> Lovely the woods, waters, meadows, combes,* vales,
> All the air things wear that build this world of Wales;
> Only the inmate does not correspond:
> God, lover of souls, swaying considerate scales,
> Complete thy creature dear O where it fails,
> Being mighty a master,† being a father and fond.

* The wooded hills and meadow lands.
† Transpose, "Being a mighty Master"

This is essentially the same prayer as he had uttered in "The Wreck of the Deutschland" ("Father and fondler of heart thou hast wrung . . . melt him but master him still").

The culmination of "The Loss of the Eurydice" is another variation on this theme. Most of the elegy is a pictorial description and narration of the wreck of the boat and the loss of lives. But at the close the poet cannot restrain himself and he bursts out:

> O well wept, mother have lost son;
> Wept, wife; wept, sweetheart would be one:
>   Though grief yield them no good
> Yet shed what tears sad truelove should.
>
> But to Christ lord of thunder
> Crouch; lay knee by earth low under:
>   "Holiest, loveliest, bravest,
> Save my hero, O Hero savest.
>
> And the prayer thou hearst me making
> Have, at the awful overtaking,
>   Heard; have heard and granted,
> Grace that day grace was wanted."

For Robert Bridges, apparently disturbed by the elliptical compression of these lines, the poet wrote an exegesis which makes the prayer essentially the same as that of "In the Valley of the Elwy":

> The words are put into the mouth of a mother, wife, or sweetheart who has lost a son, husband, or lover respectively by the disaster and who prays Christ, whom she addresses "Hero, savest", that is, "Hero that savest", that is, Hero of a Saviour, to save (that is, have saved) her hero, that is, her son, husband, or lover: "Hero of a Saviour" (the line means) "be the saviour of my hero".[7]

There is the same hope expressed in "The Wreck of the Deutschland" that grace will have saved the souls which often seem to reject it:

> Yet did the dark side of the bay* of thy blessing
> Not vault them, the millions of rounds of thy mercy not reeve† even
>   them in?

---

* Probably the architectural as well as the geographical figure is implied.
† Dialect word signifying inclusion.

Such too is the burden of "The Lantern out of Doors", written contemporaneously with "The Loss of the Eurydice" and "In the Valley of the Elwy".

> Christ minds; Christ's interest, what to avow or amend
>   There, éyes them, heart wánts, care háunts, foot fóllows kind,
> Their ránsom, thèir rescue, ánd first, fást, last friend.

"In the Valley of the Elwy" had spoken of the beauty of Wales; "only the inmate does not correspond". The contrast between nature as symbolic of innocence and man's tendency to sin is the basis of a further poem, "Spring". Into the octet of this sonnet Hopkins poured all his keen sensibility, sketching the natural beauty and freshness of Spring:

> Nothing is so beautiful as spring—
>   When weeds, in wheels, shoot long and lovely and lush;
>   Thrush's eggs look little low heavens, and thrush
> Through the echoing timber does so rinse and wring
> The ear, it strikes like lightnings to hear him sing;
>   The glassy peartree leaves and blooms, they brush
>   The descending blue; that blue is all in a rush
> With richness; the racing lambs too have fair their fling.

This becomes reminiscent of an earlier sinless world, of Eden, when natural beauty and moral beauty existed side by side, when all created things, creatures and man, were praising God and giving Him glory:

> What is all this juice and all this joy?
>   A strain of the earth's sweet being in the beginning
> In Eden garden.

Then comes the closing prayer or admonition to win innocent and sinless youth, Christ's choice, before it "sour with sinning"—while it still has moral beauty:

> Have, get, before it cloy,
> Before it cloud, Christ, lord, and sour with sinning,
> Innocent mind and Mayday in girl and boy
> Most, O maid's child, thy choice and worthy the winning.

It is just because—and this is to be remembered all through these poems—man is free that he can sin; it is just because he is free that he can refuse to use nature sacramentally, can turn his back on the call to the Cross, can refuse to follow Christ. And Hopkins wrote a magnificent poem on the nature of man. "The Caged Skylark".

Constituted by a substantial union of body and soul, man must use his will, which distinguishes him from the rest of creation, to mould himself to perfection, a perfection in which body and soul cooperate according to the nature of their union. He is not soul alone, with the body a mere instrument, as Plato would have it. Man is not man without the body. That body is not a prison which only hampers the soul. Man is not to try, in a false sort of spirituality, to throw off the body, the senses. St. Thomas contended that the soul, being an integral part of the human composition, is constituted in its full natural perfection only by its union with the body. Indeed, he taught that "even after death, when the soul attains its beatitude in the vision of God, 'its desire is not fully set at rest': it longs for reunion with the body as partner in its glory".[8]

Man himself is a hierarchy of powers, each important, yet to be subordinated one to another. Man, since the fall in the Garden of Eden, has had to practise asceticism, "to make sensuality", as St. Ignatius expressed it in the Spiritual Exercises, "obey reason and all inferior parts be more subject to the superior". The life of the senses, however, must not be suppressed or killed; it must be controlled and dedicated.

These are the ideas which Hopkins endeavoured to communicate in "The Caged Skylark", which deals with the nature of man, on the scholastic theory of the substantial union of body and the spirit according to which the body and the senses cannot be rejected but must be disciplined, because "Man's spirit will be flesh-bound when found at best, But uncumbered".

The major part of the poem expresses the difficulties of living in the body, of obtaining the perfect equipoise:

As a dare-gale skylark scanted in a dull cage
    Man's mounting spirit in his bone-house, mean house, dwells—
    That bird beyond the remembering his free fells;
This in drudgery, day-labouring-out life's age.

Though aloft on turf or perch or poor low stage,
    Both sing sometimes the sweetest, sweetest spells,
    Yet both droop deadly sometimes in their cells
Or wring their barriers in bursts of fear or rage.

Not that the sweet-fowl, song-fowl, needs no rest—
Why, hear him, hear him, babble and drop down to his nest,
    But his own nest, wild nest, no prison.

Such lines would seem to consider the flesh as a cage, a prison
for the soul, the spirit anxious to find freedom from its bondage.
But the final lines make clear that this is true only until the ideal
relationship (when the cage is no cage, the prison no prison) is
attained:

Man's spirit will be flesh-bound when found at best,
But uncumbered: meadow-down is not distressed*
For a rainbow footing it nor he for his bones risen.

And the dogmas of the Incarnation, the Resurrection, as well as
the whole liturgical worship of the Church, have constantly re-
asserted the sanctity of the body, the holiness of the senses.

"The Windhover: To Christ our Lord" is the greatest of
Hopkins' poems of this period, greatest in the implications of
its subject, greatest in its metrical accomplishment. Hopkins
himself referred to it as "the best thing I ever wrote".[9] It is
indeed "the achieve of, the mastery of the thing".

The octet is an onomatopoeic and empathic recreation of the
flight of the windhover in its magnificent and triumphant career.
Instrumental in its music, it moves with the rhythm of flight: it
starts with a swirl, soars, whirls again, and then banks with the
wind:

I caught this morning morning's minion, king-
    dom of daylight's dauphin, dapple-dawn-drawn Falcon,†
        in his riding
    Of the rolling level underneath him steady air, and striding
High there, how he rung upon the rein‡ of a wimpling wing
In his ecstasy! then off, off forth on swing,
    As a skate's heel sweeps smooth on a bow-bend: the hurl and
        gliding
    Rebuffed the big wind. My heart in hiding
Stirred for a bird,—the achieve of, the mastery of the thing!

---

* i.e. A meadow no more feels the pressure, the discomfort, of the rainbow
which rests on it than the new man feels his body.

†The windhover is the kestrel, the small European falcon noted for its habit
of hovering in the air against the wind.

‡ As I. A. Richards has suggested, "a term from the *manège*, ringing of a
horse—causing it to circle round on a long rein".

From the opening "I caught this morning morning's minion" to "the achieve of, the mastery of the thing" the poet is in an ecstasy of amazement at the mastery and brilliant success of the wind-hover—a beauty so great that it is difficult to imagine any that has its equal.

But there is a beauty far, far greater. And the sestet is devoted to a revelation of a beauty beyond this beauty, a beauty which is "a billion times told lovelier, more dangerous" than the purely natural and triumphant flight. And whence comes this achievement which is more than achievement, this mastery which is more than mastery?

It is in the act of "buckling", when the windhover swoops down, when its flight is crumpled, when "brute beauty and valour and act, oh, air, pride, plume" in an act of self-sacrifice, of self-destruction, of mystical self-immolation send off a fire far greater than any natural beauty:

> Brute beauty and valour and act, oh, air, pride, plume, here
> Buckle! And the fire that breaks from thee then, a billion
> Times told lovelier, more dangerous, O my chevalier!

Nor is this to be wondered at, for this is true even in humble little things—is true of everything: the sheen of common earth shines out when the plough breaks it into furrows; and fire breaks from fire only in the moment of its own destruction:

> No wonder of it: shéer plód makes plough down sillion*
> Shine, and blue-bleak embers, ah my dear,
> Fall, gall themselves, and gash gold-vermilion.

Here is Christ upon the Cross and Hopkins the *alter Christus*. Beautiful was Christ's public life, but "a billion times told lovelier" was His self-immolation on the Cross, His sacrifice transmuted by the Fire of Love into something far greater than any mere natural beauty. More beautiful than any natural achievement was Hopkins' own humble and plodding continuance of the ethic of redemption through his own mystical self-destruction, his own humble following of Christ to the very Cross of Calvary. And the beauty of Christ and the beauty of the Jesuit to eyes that see more than this world is the beauty of their dying to live. "Here the faithful waver, the faithless fable and miss." But always

---

* Furrow (Fr. *sillon*).

           thou art above, thou Orion of light;
    Thy unchancelling poising palms were weighing the worth,
        Thou martyr-master: in thy sight
  Storm flakes were scroll-leaved flowers, lily showers—sweet heaven
  was astrew in them.

This is the story of Christ and it is the story of Gerard Manley Hopkins: The Folly of the Cross.

Priest and Preacher: 1877–81

BUT Gerard Manley Hopkins had not entered the Society of Jesus to be a poet. During the four years following his ordination he filled various posts until he went back to Roehampton, in October, 1881, for his tertianship. He was, of course, subject to obedience to his religious superiors: it was for them to decide the station in which he would be most likely to contribute to "the greater glory of God".

He was shifted often. "Permanence with us", he wrote to Bridges, "is ginger-bread permanence; cob-web, soapsud, and frost-feather permanence".[1] For a few months he was Select Preacher at the Jesuits' Farm Street Church in London. Then he left for Mount St. Mary's College, Chesterfield, to become its "sub-minister" or bursar. Then for almost a year he preached in Oxford, at St. Aloysius' principally, but also elsewhere. At St. Aloysius' may be seen the holy water font dedicated to his memory, the tribute of Baron de Paravicini, who was an undergraduate friend and later Fellow of Balliol, and of his wife.

For a short time after he left his post at Oxford and before taking his station as preacher at St. Francis Xavier's at Liverpool, he was temporarily on the staff at St. Joseph's, Bedford Leigh, near Manchester. His Liverpool appointment was followed by one to St. Joseph's, Glasgow.

He did not have more than mediocre success as a preacher, though his superiors tried hard to find a congenial post for him. But this must not be interpreted as implying that he was a failure as a Jesuit, for sanctity is, after all, the ultimate criterion of the success of a follower of St. Ignatius, and sanctity is not to be judged in terms of an obvious effectiveness—no more than Christ himself is to be so judged.

Wherever he was, he found the endless routine of parish duties trying. "The parish work of Liverpool", he confessed to Canon Dixon, "is very wearying to mind and body and leaves me nothing but odds and ends of time". And again he wrote: "Liverpool is of all places the most museless. It is indeed a most unhappy and miserable spot. There is moreover no time for writing anything serious."[2]

To one of Hopkins' temperament, to one who so deeply loved

natural beauty and found Wales "a mother of Muses", Leigh,
Liverpool, and Glasgow were depressing: "You cannot tell", he
said, "what a slavery of mind . . . it is to live my life in a great
town."[3]

The effects of nineteenth-century industrialism he found re-
volting. To his friend Alexander Baillie he wrote:

> What I dislike in towns and in London in particular is the
> misery of the poor; the dirt, squalor, and the ill-shapen degraded
> physical (putting aside moral) type of so many of the people, with
> the deeply dejecting, unbearable thought that by degrees almost all
> our population will become a town population and a puny, un-
> healthy and cowardly one.[4]

Yet Hopkins was not Pharisaic or unsympathetic; but he admitted
that he did "dearly like calling a spade a spade".[5] What man had
made of man he recognized. In writing to Canon Dixon about
Cobbett's History of the Reformation he says once more what he
wrote to Baillie:

> The most valuable part of it to me is the doctrine about the
> origin of pauperism. I should much myself like to follow this out.
> My Liverpool and Glasgow experience laid upon my mind a con-
> viction, a truly crushing conviction, of the misery of town life to
> the poor and more than to the poor, of the misery of the poor in
> general, of the degradation even of our race, of the hollowness of
> this century's civilization.

And he added a note which indicates the depth of his feeling: "It
made even life a burden to me to have daily thrust upon me the
things I saw."[6]

Such a passage as the following reminds one of St. Stanislaus
or St. Philip Neri who became physically ill in the presence of a
corrupt soul:

> I daresay you have long expected as you have long deserved
> an answer. . . . But I never could write; time and spirits were
> wanting; one is so fagged, so harried and gallied up and down.
> And the drunkards go on drinking, the filthy, as the scripture
> says, are filthy still; human nature is so inveterate.[7]

This sensitivity to moral ugliness increases with his active priesthood. And yet his religion made him see another side: while it
make him realize how deeply sin was responsible for the sordidness of things about him, at the same time it showed him by con-

trast what man should be. This is forcefully expressed in a
letter in which he speaks of   the difference the apprehension of
the Catholic truths one after another makes in one's views of
everything".[8] He goes on to apply this:

> You will no doubt understand what I mean by saying that the
> *sordidness* of things, which one is compelled perpetually to
> feel, is perhaps, taking *ἐν ἀνθ᾽ ἑνός*, the most unmixedly
> painful thing one knows of: and this is (objectively) intensified
> and (subjectively) destroyed by Catholicism. If people could all
> know this, to take no higher ground, no other inducement would
> to very many minds be needed to lead them to Catholicism and no
> opposite inducement could dissuade them from it.[9]

The contrast between things as they are and as they ought to be!
Catholicism darkens the view of the world because it is seen as
it is, and yet it gives a new vision, a vision of the world as it
should be.

Hopkins would not have been a follower of Ignatius if his
primary concern had not been with the souls of men. However
wearying were his parish duties and however depressing the
ugliness of nineteenth-century civilization ("fast foundering own
generation"), and however disheartening the museless dreariness
of his life, yet Hopkins drew comfort and consolation at times
from his only hope: the fervency of his flock. "I have left Oxford", he tells Bridges from Bedford Leigh:

> I am appointed to Liverpool, I do not know for what work,
> but am in the meantime supplying at the above address. Leigh is a
> town smaller and with less dignity than Rochdale [where Bridges
> lived] and in a flat; the houses red, mean, and two-storied; there
> are a dozen mills or so, and coal-pits also; the air is charged with
> smoke as well as damp; but the people are hearty. Now at
> Oxford every prospect pleases and only man is vile, I mean un-
> satisfactory to a Catholic missioner. I was yesterday at St.
> Helens, probably the most repulsive place in Lancashire or out
> of the Black Country. The stench of sulphuretted hydrogen rolls
> in the air and films of the same gas form on railing and pave-
> ment.[10]

Here the poet is revolted by the sordidness of Leigh, yet the
priest's heart goes out to the souls of men. To Canon Dixon he
said much the same thing: "The place is very gloomy but our
people hearty and devoted."[11]

These are the very materials out of which his poems of this period

were made. Man had sinned, turned away from God, had mis-
used the created things which God had placed in the world to
bring man to Him—man was sinking back into the slime from
which God had raised him. Thus "The Sea and the Skylark":

> How these two shame this shallow and frail tow.
> How ring right out our sordid turbid time,
> Being pure! We, life's pride and cared-for crown,
>
> Have lost that cheer and charm of earth's past prime:
> Our make and making break, are breaking, down
> To man's last dust, drain fast towards man's first slime.

And in "God's Grandeur" he pleads:

> Why do men then now not reck his rod?
> Generations have trod, have trod, have trod;
> And all is seared with trade; bleared, smeared with toil;
> And wears man's smudge and shares man's smell.

No wonder he had prayed: "Complete thy creature dear O where
it fails." The concern of the priest for the salvation of man is in
such poems—and this concern is the very life of the sermons he
preached during these years.

The principal norm for judging a sermon is its effectiveness
with its particular audience. Delightful as we may find the reading of Hopkins' sermons—and they do give a peculiar pleasure of
their own—we must realize that the sermon is meant to be delivered, and some of the qualities which make for good reading
are not necessarily effective in the pulpit.

Apparently his sermons varied in their effectiveness. One that
he preached in the novitiate on St. Stanislaus, the patron of Jesuit
novices, was long remembered by his contemporaries in the
Order. On the other hand, he had several almost disastrous experiences. To a "Dominical", that is, a practice sermon, which he
delivered as a seminarian on the text: "Then Jesus said: Make the
men sit down" (John vi, 10), he appended the note:

> This was a Dominical and was delivered on Mid-Lent Sunday,
> 11th March, 1877, as far as the blue pencilmark on the sheet
> before this. People laughed at it prodigiously, I saw some of them
> roll on their chairs with laughter. This made me lose the thread,
> so that I did not deliver the last two paragraphs right but mixed
> things up. The last paragraph, in which *Make the men sit down*

is often repeated, far from having a good effect, made them roll more than ever.[12]

It should be explained that a "Dominical" is not preached in the chapel, but during dinner, where the audience of fellow-seminarians is apt to be either very hardened and unconcerned or very critical; further, conditions under which such a trial sermon is given are such that the "circumstantial laugh" may easily occur. Still it is true that in a sermon the line between genuine effectiveness and bathos is a very thin one.

Voice and delivery are so important in the pulpit that with their aid even poor material will take fire, and with their absence the best material becomes trivial and monotonous. Unfortunately we know almost nothing about these elements in Hopkins' sermons. But we do know that he was sometimes confused and nervous. After he had been preaching almost a year we find him admitting to Bridges, who had apparently gone to hear him:

> Next Sunday's sermon must be learnt better than last's. I was very little nervous at the beginning and not at all after. It was pure forgetting and flurry. The delivery was not good, but I hope to get a good one in time. I shall welcome any criticisms which are not controversy.[13]

But such difficulties apparently continued, for after two years of experience we find him jotting in his sermon-book: "The first 6 paragraphs I delivered confusedly and the last I added in preaching and have written since."[14]

His superiors apparently had advised him to write out his sermons beforehand to give him fluidity. But at least once he became discouraged by this procedure. In his book of sermons he started: "Notes (for it seems that written sermons do no good)." Then follows a paragraph of rough notes; but after a dozen lines he writes, "However the Rector wishes me to write", thinks better of the matter, and completes the draft of a sermon on the Paraclete.[15] For us it is, of course, fortunate that he did write out many of his sermons. Some twenty-seven have survived in whole or part; six have found their way into print.

One genuinely pathetic note is entered in the book apropos of a sermon he had preached at Liverpool one July evening in 1880:

> I preached also the Friday before, but at half an hour's notice and have no notes. The sermon was made out of an old one in this book and was on our Lord's fondness for praising and re-

warding people. I thought people must be quite touched by this consideration and that I even saw some wiping their tears, but when the same thing happened next week I perceived that it was hot and that it was sweat they were wiping away.[16]

He records after this sermon that one of his penitents admitted that he had slept through parts of it.

Such experiences must have been disheartening   And the sermons show a constant effort to appeal to his audience. There is great orderliness in all of them, a logical schematic development which makes lucid reading.   But often the sermons suggest the class-room treatise or disputation.   And he has indeed a fondness for making distinctions which are not difficult to follow in print but which would put too great a strain on the attention and application of a Lancashire congregation. His love of truth was so exacting that he could let few statements go unqualified.

He seems to have realized that his sermons were difficult for the ear to follow, for he has these revealing words to say in one of them:

> Bend then, my brethren, your ears and minds to follow and understand, for it is the Church that has appointed the words to be read and not for nothing, not for us to stare or sleep over them but to heed them and take their meaning; besides that it seems to me a contemptible and unmanly thing, for men whose minds are naturally clear, to give up at the first hearing of a hard passage in the Scripture and in the holiest of all kinds of learning to care to know no more than children know.[17]

His efforts to be simple and to adapt his thought to the level of his audience account both for much of their peculiar charm as well as for the difficulties he got into.

There is, of course, no originality of doctrine, but there is an element of daring in the means Hopkins employs to make himself understood. In his efforts to translate theology into terms understandable to his Lancashire congregation he will employ analogies and similes which may prove shocking to those who have never comprehended the application of theology to everyday life and experience. In one of his sermons he said:

> God heeds all things at once. He takes more interest in a merchant's business than the merchant, in a vessel's steering than the pilot, in a lover's sweetheart than the lover, in a sick man's pain than the sufferer, in our salvation than we ourselves.[18]

—The ideas are thoroughly sound and orthodox; but such an
application may have been disconcerting to his audience. And we
know it was to his rector, for in Hopkins' sermon-book on the
left-hand page, opposite the text, he wrote:

> In consequence of this word *sweetheart* I was in a manner
> suspended and at all events forbidden (it was some time after)
> to preach without having my sermon revised. However when I
> was going to take the next sermon I had to give after this regula-
> tion came into force to Fr. Clare for revision he poopoohed the
> matter and would not look at it.[19]

He often tries to bring home to his congregation the implications of some idea in terms of their own experience. To do this
he often employs homely comparisons at some length. One of
the most vivid in its effectiveness occurs in a sermon on the
Paraclete. First he tells what a Paraclete is, translating a dozen
times so as to define in terms of ordinary experience:

> But what is a Paraclete? Often it is translated Comforter, but a
> Paraclete does more than comfort. The word is Greek; there is
> no one English word for it and no one Latin word, *Comforter*
> is not enough. A Paraclete is one who comforts, who cheers, who
> encourages, who persuades, who exhorts, who stirs up, who
> urges forward, who calls on; what the spur and word of command
> is to a horse, what clapping of hands is to a speaker, what a
> trumpet is to the soldier, that a Paraclete is to the soul: *one who
> calls us on*, that is what it means, a Paraclete is one who calls us
> on to good.[20]

Then having defined a Paraclete in these terms, he presents a
final extended comparison, homely and exuberant:

> One sight is before my mind, it is homely but it comes home:
> you have seen at cricket how when one of the batsmen at the
> wicket has made a hit and wants to score a run . . . how eagerly
> the first will cry: Come on, come on!—a Paraclete is just that,
> something that cheers the spirit of man, with signals and with
> cries, all zealous that he should do something and full of assur-
> ance that if he will he can, calling him on, springing to meet
> him half way, crying to his ears or to his heart: This way to do
> God's will, this way to save your soul, come on, come on![21]

One would imagine that such a comparison would appeal
strongly to Liverpool factory hands. Yet is is also easy to imagine
that poor delivery might have made it bathetic. But sometimes

he is genuinely successful as where, in a sermon on the Fall of Man, he draws a parallel between the kingdom of God and an earthly commonwealth.

Occasionally his similes did become obviously bizarre. To make clear that the visible Church is the organism for transmitting grace to those who approach it willingly, he compared it to a cow with full udders, wandering through the pastures of the world, ready to nourish any one who came to milk it. And this before the London congregation of the Jesuits' Farm Street Church! No wonder his contemporary in the Order who tells the story adds: "But great genius must be excused eccentricities."

And this genius which Hopkins had, making him see reality as few others had seen it, and also making him suffer as few have suffered, is a genius, whether in the pulpit or in poetry, which shocked conventional sensibilities. The metaphor of the cow was of a piece with any number of the metaphors in his poems. His eccentric delight in the long cumulative lists in his sermons is no more singular than such lines from "The Wreck of the Deutschland" as:

> Pride, rose, prince, hero of us, high-priest,
> Our hearts' charity's hearth's fire, our thoughts' chivalry's throng's
> Lord.

With a similar crescendo he brings to a conclusion one of his most delightful sermons sketching Christ as the model and perfect man:

> Take some time to think of him; praise him in your hearts. You can over your work or on your road praise him, saying over and over again: Glory be to Christ's body; Glory to the body of the Word made flesh; Glory to the body suckled at the Blessed Virgin's breasts; Glory to Christ's body in its beauty; Glory to Christ's body in its weariness; Glory to Christ's body in its Passion, death and burial; Glory to Christ's body risen; Glory to Christ's body in the Blessed Sacrament; Glory to Christ's soul; Glory to his genius and wisdom; Glory to his unsearchable thoughts; Glory to his saving words; Glory to his sacred heart; Glory to its courage and manliness; Glory to its meekness and mercy; Glory to its every heartbeat, to its joys and sorrows, wishes, fears; Glory in all things to Jesus Christ.[22]

In an effort to make his congregation understand that the Sacred Heart is Christ under the aspect of His love for us, he uses— in a passage too long to quote here—a whole page of hearts to impress his audience. His strain at simplicity not infrequently resulted in the vice of over-elaboration.

But there are few of the defects one often finds in sermons. He was not satisfied with superficialities and never with pious rhetoric and platitudes. He uses rhetorical devices like parallelism and balance, but they do not become mechanical and never so poundingly monotonous that they become obvious. Seldom is he so formal in his rhetoric as in this period descriptive of Christ: "Poor was his station, laborious his life, bitter his ending: through poverty, through labour, through crucifixion his majesty of nature more shines."[23]

His pictorial skill and dramatic effectiveness in reconstructing scenes, his concreteness and use of all the senses—which are so pervasive in his poetry—these one can most easily observe within the general framework of ideas which form the subject-matter of his sermons.

It is not surprising that many of the ideas as well as methods of development and progression are drawn from the Spiritual Exercises. He did not slavishly follow St. Ignatius' directions and suggestions, themselves very flexible; rather the Exercises gave to his own thoughts a channel for expression. Anxious as he was to fulfil the Ignatian ideal himself, as a shepherd and priest he necessarily wished to help others on the same difficult road. In his sermons the confessor's care of souls is in every admonition, in every exhortation that each one himself become an *alter Christus*.

The "Foundation and Principle" became the cornerstone of his sermons. "Man was created", he preached, paraphrasing St. Ignatius,

> To praise, honour, and serve God, thus fulfilling God's desire in bringing him into being, and by so doing to save his soul, thus fulfilling his own desire, the desire of everything that has being. He was created to give God glory and by so doing to win himself glory.[24]

Having set forth his thesis, Hopkins proceeds to show in his sermons how man by sinning has failed to fulfil his purpose. He follows the order of the Spiritual Exercises in presenting the picture of Adam and Eve's loss of original innocence. The First Week of the Exercises asks the exercitant to contemplate the first sin in the Garden of Eden. St. Ignatius constantly urges the retreatant to reconstruct the scene, "to see the persons . . . to look, mark and contemplate what they are saying . . . to look and consider what they are doing . . . to hear with the hearing what they are, or might be talking about". Always he suggests the application of the five senses to the reconstruction of the scene, which he calls "a composition, seeing the place". (And this may be done throughout the Exercises, for the entire life of Christ, etc. Note once more how St. Ignatius, too, urged the use of the senses.)

That is exactly the method which Hopkins employs in many of his sermons. When he wishes to talk to his parishioners about the sin of our first parents, for instance, he paints a picture of Eden, dramatizes Adam and Eve in it, sketches their actions, and gives them speech; constantly he applies the five senses in reconstructing the scene in its fullness. Here is the serpent:

> Now, brethren, fancy, as you may, that rich tree all laden with its shining fragrant fruit and swaying down from one of its boughs, as the pythons and great snakes of the East do now, waiting for their prey to pass and then to crush it, swaying like a long spray of vine or the bine of a great creeper, not terrible but beauteous, lissome, marked with quaint streaks and eyes or flushed with rainbow colours, the Old Serpent. We must suppose he offered her the fruit, as though it were the homage and the tribute of the brute to man, of the subject to his queen, presented it with his mouth or swept it from the boughs down before her feet; and she declined it. Then came those studied words. . . .[25]

And Satan speaks. This is a mere sample. There is a marvellous picture of Eve and analysis of her thoughts and feelings. And throughout Hopkins uses his pictorial skill and dramatic ability so as to make concrete his great scenes of Christian tradition. Occasionally he becomes so concrete and minutely circumstantial as to become almost ludicrous, but usually such qualities are controlled.

Original sin, the initial refusal of man to glorify God, becomes increasingly important in Hopkins' explanation of man's waywardness. It is in "The Wreck of the Deutschland", where man is "unteachably after evil"; through the poems of 1877-8 the emphasis on man's failure to glorify God carries the implications of this doctrine. In his later poems he will often mourn, "corruption was the world's first woe".

Several of his sermons deal with the results of this first sin. The worst effect "is concupiscence, that is to say a readiness to commit sin".[26] In an apt analogy Hopkins compares man to a watch and concupiscence to the mainspring:

> A watch wound up but kept from going has the spring always on the strain though no motion comes of it. Such a mainspring of evil in us is the concupiscence that comes in with original sin and lasts even when original sin has been taken away by baptism.[27]

Because she alone was spared "the blight man was born for", Hopkins frequently paid homage to the Blessed Virgin Mary. In many of his poems he honours her sinlessness; and he tells his people in a sermon on the Immaculate Conception, "We cannot copy our Blessed Lady in being conceived immaculate, but we can copy her in the virtues by which she became her privilege and her privilege became her".[28] Can we forget the tall nun of "The Wreck of the Deutschland" whose cry to Christ was like another advent?

> Jesu, heart's light,
> Jesu, maid's son,
> What was the feast followed the night
> Thou hadst glory of this nun?—
> Feast of the one woman without stain.
> For so conceivéd, so to conceive thee is done;
> But here was heart-throe, birth of a brain,
> Word, that heard and kept thee and uttered thee outright.

Indeed, one of the things he most prized in Scotus was that great theologian's early defence of the doctrine of the Immaculate Conception: "Who fired France for Mary without spot" ("Duns Scotus's Oxford"). In a sermon he offered a commentary (the sermon was written later than the poem) on this very passage.

Anyone who over-emphasizes man's Fall without recognizing the Christian doctrine of his redemption is bound to take a pessimistic view of the world. But Hopkins' most powerful emphasis, in his sermons as well as in his poems, is on the Incarnation and Redemption.

The "greatest event" in the history of man, he preached, is that event which undid the Fall of Man: the crucifixion and man's Redemption. This optimistic note runs through his sermons offering man hope and joy. The graces of the Redemption flood the world.

The sermons have an active and positive spirit about them. While Hopkins is always cognizant of man's tendency to commit sin, he is far more vitally concerned with building up a model of perfection and of positive virtues. The Spiritual Exercises had set up Christ as the great example.

With loving-kindness Hopkins in his sermons sets up Christ as Man as the perfect model for men. His most beautiful and haunting sermon presents Christ as "a hero all the world wants". "There met in Jesus Christ all things that can make man lovely and loveable."[11] And he sketches the hierarchy of beauties that met in Christ. "In his body he was most beautiful", says the poet-priest who was always attracted by physical beauty; some, indeed, will be shocked by the confession he makes when he says:

> In his Passion all this strength was spent, this lissomness crippled, this beauty wrecked, this majesty beaten down. But now it is more than all restored, and for myself I make no secret I look forward with eager desire to seeing the matchless beauty of Christ's body in the heavenly light.[30]

Here he reasserts once more the goodness of the body, of the senses—and this goodness has its ultimate explanation and elevation in the Incarnate Word.

Then he sketches the beauty of Christ's mind, and finally, "far higher than beauty of the body, higher than genius and wisdom the beauty of the mind, comes the beauty of his character, his character as man".[31]

This emphasis on the God-Man as the pattern, the hero, for each of us is one of Hopkins' most attractive themes. He may have been influenced by Scotus, who in his Christology liked to stress the human element, while in general St. Thomas liked to stress the divine. Some measure of Hopkins' vivid "feeling into" theology may be gained from a letter he wrote to Bridges concerning Christ and the Trinity. It is a long letter but it re-enforces what he has been busy saying in his poems and in his sermons:

> There are three persons, each God and each the same, the one, the only God: to some people this is a "dogma", a word they almost chew, that is an equation in theology, the dull algebra of schoolmen; to others it is news of their dearest friend or friends, leaving them all their lives balancing whether they have three heavenly friends or one—not that they have any doubt on the subject, but that their knowledge leaves their minds swinging; poised, but on the quiver. And this might be the ecstasy of interest,

one would think. So too of the Incarnation, a mystery less incomprehensible, it is true: to you it comes to: Christ is in some sense
God, in some sense he is not God—and your interest is in the uncertainty; to the Catholic it is: Christ is in every sense God and in
every sense man, and the interest is in the locked and inseparable
combination, or rather it is in the person in whom the combination
has its place. Therefore we speak of Christ's life as the mystery
of the Nativity, the mystery of the Crucifixion and so on of a host;
the mystery being always the same, that the child in the manger
is God, the culprit on the gallows God, and so on. Otherwise,
birth and death are not mysteries, nor is it any great mystery that
a just man should be crucified, but that God should fascinates—
with the interest of awe, of pity, of shame, of every harrowing
feeling. But I have said enough.[32]

In Hopkins' sermons, as in his poems and in his own life, religious truths are not equations in theology, "the dull algebra of
schoolmen"; they are indeed views of his dearest "friend or
friends" (did he not call the whole world "news of God"?) in
which an "ecstasy of interest" gives vitality to all he did and
thought and wrote and said.

The sermons form an integral part of all he was thinking and
feeling. Frequently what he says in his poems appears again in
his sermons; sometimes what first finds utterance in the pulpit is
later transmuted into poetry. In 1878 he had elliptically expressed in "The Loss of the Eurydice" what was later to become
part of a sermon:

> But to Christ lord of thunder
> Crouch; lay knee by earth low under:
> "Holiest, loveliest, bravest,
> Save my hero, O Hero savest. . . ."

In a sermon a year later he preached:

> Our Lord Jesus Christ, my brethren, is our hero, a hero all
> the world wants. . . . Often mothers make a hero of a son; girls of a
> sweetheart and good wives of a husband. . . . But Christ, he is the
> hero.[33]

That this is precisely the idea embedded in the lines from the
poem is unmistakeable from the explanatory letter to Bridges that
we have already seen in connection with the poem.

One of the most winning passages of this same sermon on
Christ as perfect man—a passage which stresses Him as one Who

loves to praise and reward rather than as "lord of thunder"—was the material of a poem composed six years later, "The Soldier".

The interaction between his sermons and his poems was obviously very deep. The path of influence was not in one direction: sermon might influence poem or the reverse might happen. Indeed, at times apparently both were being composed at once; for in a reference to a poem of 1888, "That Nature is a Heraclitean Fire and of the comfort of the Resurrection", Hopkins informed Bridges:

> I will now go to bed, the more so as I am going to preach to-morrow and put plainly to a Highland congregation of Mac-Donalds, MacIntoshes, MacKillops, and the rest what I am putting not at all so plainly to the rest of the world, or rather to you and Canon Dixon, in a sonnet in sprung rhythm with two codas.[24]

Such was the integration of preacher and priest attained by Gerard Manley Hopkins. His poems had been moulded and shaped by his personal practice of the Spiritual Exercises, while in his sermons he had sought more directly to mould the souls of his penitents to the same ideal of service to God. All were expressions of the same man and of the same effort.

Poems, Tertianship, More Poems (1879-83)

THE central themes of the poems of 1877-78 which Hopkins felt free to compose have already been sketched. Between 1879 and the time Hopkins entered his Tertian-ship in 1881 he added sixteen more to his body of verse. There is a distinct shift in emphasis which justifies the chronological treatment we have been pursuing, awkward as it often is. These later poems are not primarily concerned with a sacramental view of nature. They do not chant the praises of the One ablaze in the many. No, the recurrent emphasis of the poems of 1879-81 is more closely related to his previous experience of the waywardness of man. But now his poems are more than ever concerned directly with man. They are the poems of his priesthood. The priestly spirit which appears in almost all these poems is the distinguishing mark of the group. The confessor's care for souls gives temper and unity to these reforgings of priestly experience in the active ministry. After reading the poems of this period one is not surprised that one of his Jesuit contemporaries should have written of him:

> I think the characteristics in him that most struck and edified all of us who knew him were, first, what I should call his priestly spirit; this showed itself not only in the reverential way he performed his sacred duties, and spoke on sacred subjects, but his whole conduct and conversation; and secondly, his devotion and loyalty to the Society of Jesus.[1]

A new sympathy, a new tenderness, a new concern enter his poems; emotions and feelings take on a deeply attractive warmth as he moves among his people. The priest might have written of himself,

> How lovely the elder brother's
> Life all laced in the other's,
> Lóve-laced!

Most of these poems are religious in their orientation and direction. Hopkins continues to use his gift for the service of God. He himself does what, in one of the poems of this period, he urges all men to do with all of their powers:

> Take as for tool, not toy meant
> And hold at Christ's employment.

The qualities of his own genius are in these poems of his pastoral experiences with the souls of men. In one of his poems of 1879, "Henry Purcell", he says that an artist, seemingly intent on the thought he is to express, flashes off the individualizing marks of his genius:

> It is the forgéd feature finds me;* it is the rehearsal
> Of own, of abrupt self there so thrusts on, so throngs the ear.

And each of the poems of this period is stamped with Hopkins and " meaning motion fans fresh our wits with wonder".

The tenderness and concern of the priest, his duties and consolations, are beautifully recreated in "Felix Randal". The deep satisfaction drawn from the priesthood is in such lines as:

> This seeing the sick endears them to us, us too it endears.
> My tongue had taught thee comfort, touch had quenched thy tears,
> Thy tears that touched my heart, child, Felix, poor Felix Randal.

The same tender affection for his charges and the consolations of the priest are expressed in "The Bugler's First Communion". Felix Randal may have been one of Hopkins' Liverpool parishioners. The "bugler boy from barrack" we know to have been one of his penitents and communicants, and one may follow news of him in letters to Bridges. The poems of this period have a very circumstantial air about them. Out of his actual experience the poet wrote of the balm that came with his ministrations:

> How it dóes my heart good, visiting at that bleak hill,
> When limber liquid youth, that to all I teach
>   Yields tender as a pushed peach,
> Hies headstrong to its wellbeing of a self-wise self-will!
>
> Then though I should tread tufts of consolation
> Dáys áfter, só I in a sort deserve to
>   And do serve God to serve to
> Just such slips of soldiery Christ's royal ration.

Only in the full Catholic conception of the supernatural life of grace can such lines take on their full meaning. Man's nature has been wounded by original sin. But counteracting man's loss of

* i.e. "It is the highly individualized expression that has its impact upon me."

original innocence and grace is man's redemption through the
grace of Christ, "Christ's gift". It is through grace that man is
reunited to God. And the whole sacramental system of the
Catholic Church is designed to bring to man the grace of Christ.
It is the priest, it is Hopkins, who is the mediator. To Felix
Randal he had given Christ's "sweet reprieve and ransom", and
in the present poem he gives the Eucharist:

> There! and your sweetest sendings, ah divine,
> By it, heavens, befall him!*
>
> .   .   .   .
>
> O for now charms, arms, what bans off bad
> And locks love ever in a lad!

And the priest prays—for the poem is full of prayers—that the
boy be protected from evil:

> Frowning and forefending angel-warder
> Squander the hell-rook ranks sally to molest him;†
>   March, kind comrade, abreast him;
> Dress his days to a dexterous and starlight order.

And yet, in his priestly concern, and with his priestly experience
knowing the waywardness of man, he fears for the future of the
boy—but he also prays for him:

> But may he not rankle and roam
> In backwheels though bound home?—
> That left to the Lord of the Eucharist, I here lie by;‡
>
> Recorded only, I have put my lips on pleas
> Would brandle adamantine heaven with ride and jar, did
>   Prayer go disregarded:
> Forward-like, but however, and like favourable heaven heard these.§

The beauty of sinless youth with its days directed towards a
starlight order made a deep impression on Hopkins. "I hope to
enclose a little scene that touched me at Mount St. Mary's",
he wrote to Bridges. The "little scene" was a poem on the
beauty of natural affection between two brothers who attended

---

* i.e. May your sweetest graces, of God, flowing from the Eucharist through
Christ in heaven, fall to him.
† As Bridges has suggested: Scatter the ranks of hellish vultures that sally
to molest him.
‡ i.e. I leave to the Lord of the Eucharist his return to virtue.
§ Expresses the poet's confidence that his prayers for the youth will be
heard by heaven.

the Jesuit school where Hopkins had been bursar. This is the poem, "Brothers" (1880), which opens with the lines:

> How lovely the elder brother's
> Life all laced in the other's,
> Lóve-laced!

It closes with verses joyful with admiration at these youths:

> Ah Nature, framed in fault,
> There's comfort then, there's salt;
> Nature, bad, base, and blind,
> Dearly thou canst be kind;
> There dearly thén, deárly,
> I'll cry thou canst be kind.

The innocence of youth always drew from the priest the hope that it would be preserved in its orientation towards God. "On the Portrait of Two Beautiful Young People", written six years later, expresses the same concern. And earlier, in 1877, he had written in "Spring" of

> Innocent mind and Mayday in girl and boy,
>   Most, O maid's child, thy choice and worthy the winning.

This theme of the purity of youth, "framed in fault", that is, bearing the stain of original sin, still not yet corrupted by sins of their own, sprang from Hopkins' priestly desire to protect the innocence of his charges. One of his Jesuit contemporaries has recalled of Hopkins:

> What struck me most of all in him was his child-like guileless-ness and simplicity, his gentleness, tender-heartedness, and his loving compassion for the young, the weak, the poor, and for all who were in any trouble or distress. Joined to this and closely connected with it, was his purity of heart and shrinking dread of anything that tended to endanger, especially in the young, the angelic virtue.[2]

The years of active ministry brought more poems like "The Bugler's First Communion" and "Brothers". Like these poems, "The Handsome Heart" (1879) was drawn from his own experience. He tells Bridges the incident upon which it was based and, as in the case of the bugler, he follows the subject's progress in after life.

"The Handsome Heart" opens with the story in dialogue form:

> "But tell me, child, your choice; what shall I buy
> You?"—"Father, what you buy me I like best."
> With the sweetest air that said, still plied and pressed,
> He swung to his first poised purport of reply.

Then comes the exclamation at the heart which has opened itself
to grace:

> What the heart is! which, like carriers let fly—
> Doff darkness, homing nature knows the rest—
> To its own fine function, wild and self-instressed,
> Falls light as ten years long taught how to and why.

In the next triplet the poet sets up his hierarchy of "beauties"
—a hierarchy which he echoes in his sermons and letters:

> Mannerly-hearted! more than handsome face—
> Beauty's bearing* or muse of mounting vein,
> All, in this case, bathed in high hallowing grace. .

In his sermon on Christ as the perfect man preached during this
same year he had set up the same hierarchy. In a letter to Bridges
he established a similar scale:

> I think then no one can admire beauty of the body more than I
> do. . . . But this kind of beauty is dangerous. Then comes the
> beauty of the mind, such as genius, and this is greater than the
> beauty of the body and not to call dangerous. And more beauti-
> ful than the beauty of the mind is beauty of character, the "hand-
> some heart".[3]

The beauty of the soul, then, is superior to outward physical
beauty, though the latter is not to be snubbed; it is to be subordinated as a good, but it is not the highest perfection. The
handsome heart, "bathed in high hallowing grace", has the
highest beauty, "God's better beauty, grace", as Hopkins called
it in a later poem. Then comes the final exhortation:

> Of heaven what boon to buy you, boy, or gain
> Not granted!—Only . . . O on that path you pace
> Run all your race, O brace sterner that strain!

Mortality, a consequence of original sin, makes haste essential for
the attainment of the "handsome heart". The fall of man

---

* i.e. (More than) Beauty's bearing.

Hopkins said in his Commentary on the Spiritual Exercises, "brought in the law of decay and consumption in inanimate nature . . .moral death and original sin in the world of man".[4]

The transiency of all things brought to him its message of sadness, a message especially associated with the passing of beauty: "And beauty's dearest veriest vein is tears." This is a note that runs all through the poetry of Hopkins, as it must in any true artist who, as the author of *The Sudden Rose* suggests, "is aware in the depths of his spirit of a consuming hunger for something that the earth, despite its loveliness, cannot satisfy, and that he is never so completely a man as when he is most aware of that hunger, that nostalgic pain of his exiled heart".[5] Thus it is that Plotinus could say: This is the spirit that beauty must ever induce, wonderment and a delicious trouble, longing and love and a trembling that is all delight. The pangs of mortality are a part of all created things. In "Spring and Fall" Hopkins tells us that youth has an intuitive, almost innate knowledge of the sad transiency of all things due to the blight of original sin. Remarkably compressed and condensed, the poem opens with a tender and gentle address —the voice of the kindly father-confessor to a child:

> Márgarét, are you gríeving
> Over Goldengrove unleaving?
> Leáves, like the things of man, you
> With your fresh thoughts care for, can you?
> Ah! ás the heart grows older
> It will come to such sights colder
> By and by, nor spare a sigh
> Though worlds of wanwood* leafmeal† lie;
> And yet you will weep and know why.
> Now no matter, child, the name:
> Sórrow's springs are the same.

Continuing in his masterful sprung rhythm, the priest explains to her what she had already dimly felt:

> Nor mouth had, no nor mind, expresseu
> What heart heard of, ghost guessed:‡
> It is the blight man was born for,
> It is Margaret you mourn for.

---

* A very effective coinage.
† (*cf.* "piecemeal"). Leaf by leaf.
‡ Neither your mouth nor even your mind has expressed what your heart must have known and your spirit must have guessed.

On the use man makes of his own powers and of created things depends his eternal status; his own weakness and the transiency of his years make the call of the future life overwhelmingly important. Such is the poignancy penetrating an undated fragment:

> The telling time our task is; time's some part,
> Not all, but we were framed to fail and die—
> One spell and well that one. There, ah thereby
> Is comfort's carol of all or woe's worst smart.

No wonder then that the spiritual takes precedence over all gifts and beauties in the priest-poet's admonitions and exhortations.

Yet there is a way to arrest the transience of beauty and to give it eternal value; and that is by dedicating beauty to God in order that it may become "God's better beauty, grace". By being affirmed in God mortal beauty becomes immortal beauty. Such is the burden of "The Leaden Echo and the Golden Echo".

This is the song of the maidens in "St. Winefred's Well", a play Hopkins was working at from 1879 onwards. Fragments of the drama have survived, but "The Leaden Echo and the Golden Echo" is the most remarkable. The legend of St. Winefred is closely connected with the district of Wales in which Hopkins studied his theology: St. Beuno's was named after her uncle, and six miles away is a spring or well associated with the story of her life. Two years after Hopkins had left St. Beuno's he had started work on a tragedy concerning her life, and in 1881 he wrote the song of the maidens.

The poem has many of the qualities of song and Hopkins himself said, "I never did anything more musical".[6] With crescendo the Leaden Echo puts the opening question:

> How to kéep—is there ány, any, is there none such, nowhere known
> some, bow or brooch or braid or brace, láce, latch or catch or key
> to keep
> Back beauty, keep it, beauty, beauty, beauty, ... from vanishing away?

And it answers its own question:

> No there's none, there's none, O no there's none,

and concludes with its own echo in a diminuendo of slow despair:

> So be beginning, be beginning to despair.
> O there's none; no no no there's none:
> Be beginning to despair, to despair.

But then a beautifully lambent voice, the Golden Echo replies
—it is the religious attitude towards all gifts from God that makes
answer:

> Despair, despair, despair, despair.
>   Spare!
> There is one, yes I have one (Hush there!);
> Only not within seeing of the sun,
> Not within the singeing of the strong sun,
> Tall sun's tingeing, or treacherous the tainting of the earth's air,
> Somewhere elsewhere there is ah well where! one,
> One.

The secret, sings the Golden Echo, is to dedicate transient
beauties to the Creator:

> Resign them, sign them, seal them, send them, motion them with
>   breath,
> And with sighs soaring, soaring sighs deliver
> Them; beauty-in-the-ghost, deliver it, early now, long before death
> Give beauty back, beauty, beauty, beauty, back to God, beauty's
>   self and beauty's giver.

And the golden voice echoes from afar from the eternity of reward:

> Nay, what we had lighthanded left in surly the mere mould
> Will have waked and have waxed and have walked with the wind
>   that while we slept,
> This side, that side hurling a heavyheaded hundredfold
> What while we, while we slumbered.*

The consolation accumulates in the lines that follow:

> O then, weary then why should we tread? O why are we so
>   haggard at the heart, so care-coiled, care-killed, so fagged,
>   so fashed, so cogged, so cumbered,
> When the thing we freely forfeit is kept with fonder a care,
> Fonder a care kept than we could have kept it. . . .

Possibly in these lines we hear the painful reverberations of the
priest's anxious fear that his own attachment to beauty was at times
inordinate, that he found it "dearly and dangerously sweet" (as
he refers to it in this poem), and that he had to undergo a difficult
discipline to give it its correct place. That is not to say that he

---

* Explained in a letter in which Hopkins says that this "means 'Nay more:
the seed that we so carelessly and freely flung into the dull furrow, and then
forgot it, will have come to ear meantime!" *Letters to Bridges*, p. 156.

found it necessary to repudiate beauty. But he did dedicate his experience of beauty to God. The discipline and love that will open to the artist a vision of "God in all things and all things in God" are not easy. That is merely to say that to be a truly religious man and a truly great artist requires great strength and great love.

Dedication is the predominant motif of Hopkins' poetry as of his own life. Such is the theme of "Morning, Midday and Evening Sacrifice", which urges men to dedicate all their gifts and powers at every stage of their lives to God. In the morning, in youth:

> The dappled die-away
> Cheek and wimpled lip,
> The gold-wisp, the airy-grey
> Eye, all in fellowship—
> This, all this beauty blooming,
> This, all this freshness fuming,
> Give God while worth consuming.

And then in the midday of achievement:

> Both thought and thew now bolder
> And told by Nature: Tower;
> Head, heart, hand, heel, and shoulder
> That beat and breathe in power—
> This pride of prime's enjoyment
> Take as for tool, not toy meant
> And hold at Christ's employment.

Finally, realizing "we were framed to die" and must make haste, in the evening of maturity:

> The vault and scope and schooling
> And mastery in the mind,
> In silk-ash kept from cooling,
> And ripest under rind—
> What life half lifts the latch ⁄f,
> What hell stalks towards the snatch of,
> Your offering, with despatch, of!*

* The difficulties are explained in a letter: "I meant to compare grey hairs to the flakes of silky ash which may be seen round wood embers burnt in a clear fire and covering a 'core of heat', as Tennyson calls it. . . . 'Your offer, with despatch of' is said like 'Your ticket', 'Your reasons', 'Your money or your life', 'Your name and college': it is 'Come, your offer of all this (the matured mind), and without delay either!' (This should now explode.)" *Letters to Bridges*, p. 98.

Again the call to perfection is that found in the Spiritual Exercises, where man is asked to use all things, all created things and his own life as well, "that they may help him in prosecuting the end for which he is created . . . to praise, reverence, and serve God our Lord, and by this means to save his soul".

Two of the poems of 1879-81 are especially personal in the manner in which they express Hopkins' own interior life. The first is his prayer for Peace:

> When will you ever, Peace, wild wooddove, shy wings shut,
> Your round me roaming end, and under be my boughs?*
> When, when, Peace, will you, Peace? I'll not play hypocrite
> To own my heart:† I yield you do come sometimes; but
> That piecemeal peace is poor peace. What pure peace allows
> Alarms of wars, the daunting wars, the death of it?

And the poem ends with the chastened consolation:

> O surely, reaving Peace, my Lord‡ should leave in lieu
> Some good! And so he does leave Patience exquisite,
> That plumes to Peace thereafter. And when Peace here does house
> He comes with work to do, he does not come to coo,
>   He comes to brood and sit.

He may have prayed for peace in a scrupulous concern for his own imperfections. For one who had so resolutely such a lofty concept of spiritual perfection, the path must have been steep. The sensitivity of his own failure to root out every evil and to cultivate every virtue must have given him great anguish. "For now, after the Fall", he told his parishioners in a sermon, "good in this world is hard, it is surrounded by difficulties, the way to it lies through thorns".[7]

The priest's double duty, a duty doubly difficult, is to mould others to perfection and at the same time to strive himself to "dress his days to a dexterous and starlight order". Hopkins realized fully the teaching of the *Imitation*, a book St. Ignatius urged as supplementary to the Spiritual Exercises, that the priest especially is required to devote himself to the spiritual: "Thou hast not lightened thy burden, but art now bound by a stricter bond of discipline, and art obliged to greater perfection of sanctity."

* Transpose, "End your roaming round me, and be under my boughs".
† Transpose, "To my own heart".
‡ i.e. "O surely, my Lord, bereaving me of Peace."

"The Candle Indoors", the last poem of the 1879-81 group to be considered, turns on this difficulty. It opens with his observation of a lighted candle and two people in its light; this sight starts him musing on their life and actions:

> By that window what task what fingers ply,
> I plod wondering, a-wanting, just for lack
> Of answer the eagerer a-wanting Jessy or Jack
> There God to aggrándise, God to glorify.

But then, quickly, Hopkins turns upon himself and closes with a terrifying question that echoes all the priest's own yearning for perfection and his anguished fear that he has himself failed in himself to live up to what he expects of others. He says to his heart:

> Come you indoors, come home; your fading fire
> Mend first and vital candle in close heart's vault:
> You there are master, do your own desire;
> What hinders? Are you beam-blind, yet to a faul⁺
> In a neighbour deft-handed? are you that liar
> And, cast by conscience out, spendsavour salt?

This brings us naturally to Hopkins' Tertianship, the period during which a Jesuit turns away from his active duties as parish priest or teacher and examines his own inner life, seeking out the impure motive, or catching up any failure to practice the tenets of perfection laid down in the Spiritual Exercises and the Rules of the Society. In these terms the Constitutions of the Society outline the purposes of the Tertianship:

> Having completed the diligent task of cultivating the intellect, those who have been engaged in studies, must, during the time of the last probation, more diligently exercise themselves in the school of the heart ("in schola affectus") and devote themselves to spiritual and corporal things which help towards progress in humility and the abnegation of all sensual love as well as of their own will and judgment and also toward a greater knowledge and love of God; so that, having progressed themselves, they may better help others towards spiritual progress for the glory of God our Lord.

The Tertianship is often considered the masterpiece of St. Ignatius' programme. After several years of study or of active ministry, the Jesuit priest returns once more to a secluded life of prayer meditation, and reconsideration of the ideals of the Society. After the completion of this third year of noviceship (thus the term *Tertianship:* the Jesuit spends his first two years in the society as a novice; then come his studies, ordination, etc. and finally this third year of probation, the Tertianship) the Jesuit takes his final vows of dedication to the object of his Society: *Ad majorem Dei gloriam.*

Hopkins entered his Tertianship in October, 1881; on the feast of St. Ignatius, 31st July, 1882, he had completed this final probation. For these ten months he devoted himself to revaluation of his vocation in the Society, and to re-dedication to the ideals of the religious life.

Fortunately he was corresponding with Canon Dixon during this period. Fortunately, too, for us, Canon Dixon did not understand completely the nature of this third year of novitiate, so that Hopkins had to send him an explanation.

"So you are entering your last year of novitiate", wrote Canon Dixon, the Anglican priest, poet, and historian. "I suppose you are determined to go on with it; but it must be a severe trial—I will say no more."[8]

In replying the Jesuit corrected this impression, stated the central object of this period, and reaffirmed his devotion to the Society of Jesus:

> I see you do not understand my position in the Society. This Tertianship or Third Year of Probation or second Noviceship, for it is variously called in the Institute, is not really a noviceship at all in the sense of a time during which a candidate or probationer makes trial of our life and is free to withdraw At the end of the noviceship proper we take vows which are perpetually binding and renew them every six months (not *for* every six months but for life) till we are professed or take the final degree we are to hold, of which in the Society there are several. It is in preparation for these last vows that we make the tertianship, which is called a *schola affectus* and is meant to enable us to recover that fervour which may have cooled through application to study and contact with the world. Its exercises are however nearly the same as those of the first noviceship. As for myself, I have not only made my vows publicly some two and twenty times but make them to myself every day, so that I should be black with perjury if I drew back now. And beyond that I can say with St. Peter· To whom shall I go? *Tu verba vitae aeternae habes.*[9]

Then he adds a further revelation of his own state of mind during this period in contrast to his active ministry. "Besides all which", he says,

> My mind is here more at peace than it has ever been and I would gladly live all my life, if it were so to be, in as great or a greater seclusion from the world and be busied only with God. But in the midst of outward occupations not only the mind is drawn away from God, which may be at the call of duty and be God's will, but unhappily the will too is entangled, worldly interests freshen, and worldly ambitions revive.[10]

Here, "busied only with God", he apparently found an answer to his prayer:

> When will you ever, Peace, wild wooddove, shy wings shut,
> Your round me roaming end, and under be my boughs?

This motif of peace and content during his Tertianship runs through several letters. And in part this peace came because he suspended poetic activity; he felt, "The time is precious and will not return again and I know I shall not regret my forbearance".[11] Because the problem becomes most acute in Dublin, we shall examine in the next chapter the tension that he felt between himself as a poet and himself as a Jesuit. But, as in the case of many saintly men, he was not to know peace for any extended period. Such was not God's will for him, and Christ brought not peace but the sword.

His object during his Tertianship was, in his own words, "vacare Deo", the thrusting out of all other preoccupations and complete devotion to the spiritual life.

Some measure of the high standard by which he judged himself, of his humility and of his ardent desire for perfection is expressed in his words to Canon Dixon, in which he measured himself in relation to the ideals of St. Ignatius: "This I say: my vocation puts before me a standard so high that a higher can be found nowhere else. . . . I have never wavered in my vocation, but I have not lived up to it."[12] Such would have been the judgment of a scrupulous and heroic soul examining every intrusive motive. Judged by St. Ignatius' ideal of spiritual perfection many saints would have to say, "I have not lived up to it"—for that ideal, as we have seen, is absolute identification with Christ himself.

And that this was also the ideal which Hopkins was pursuing is forcibly emphasized during this period by the Commentary he wrote on the Spiritual Exercises.

But before we turn to that Commentary we must note a loss which is very unfortunate. During this year of Tertianship, Hopkins was also gathering material on sacrifice, for he says in a letter:

> My mind is much employed at present on the subject of Sacrifice, about which I am getting together some materials, with a view possibly to write about it some day.[13]

Whether he actually wrote on the subject we do not know, for no manuscript is extant. But from references to it in his Commentary on the Exercises it is clear that he felt that his own life must be the life of Christ being relived again, must be a life of sacrifice. With the Cross and Redemption in the background, he says, "To contribute then to that sacrifice is the end for which man was made",[14] and in another place he refers to the end of man as being "its self-sacrifice to God and its salvation".[15] To be, in a manner, Christ, was the object of Hopkins' whole life; and it was, very logically, the central theme of his Commentary on the Exercises.

In his interleaved copy of St. Ignatius' great work he kept an accumulating series of notes. These range from 1878 to 1885, but by far the larger number were written during his Tertianship. Unfortunately not all of the various notes have found their way into print.

They were apparently intended to form part of a larger project, a more complete commentary, for in a side-note on one of the interleaved pages he jotted down: "I have expressed this doctrine more clearly and correctly in the rough draft of the Commentary for the Provincial."[16] The notes are tentative, as he occasionally indicated, and often unpolished and mere jottings and notations to be later developed.

The notes are original in the sense that almost everything Hopkins wrote is original: they are daring in the means they use to get to orthodox conclusions; for Hopkins always saw reality through his own eyes, but the vision uncovered was a vision of the world in which the doctors and saints of the Church had shared. The results then can hardly be called different, but the means are often extremely individual.

Those sections which are highly speculative are frankly speculative and tentatively expressed. They deal with some of the most difficult and most controverted problems of theology—on which the Catholic mind is perfectly free to speculate, as did the mediaeval schools and the whole tradition of the Society of Jesus. And Hopkins' individuality led him to attack some of these problems from amazingly different angles—but when he finished he was where the general consensus of Catholic tradition had always been.

But he could hardly expect his Provincial to follow him in the terminology he coined—terminology which might have been lucid to Hopkins but which will be, possibly because of the undeveloped state of these notes, a stumbling-block to anyone else. He not only talks of faculty at pitch and at play, but he speaks of "faculty at splay". He writes of " 'burl' of being uncloven"; of "the doing be, the doing choose, the doing so-and-so". He speaks of an infinity of possible worlds, "each of which possible worlds and this actual one are like so many 'cleaves' or exposed faces of some pomegranate (or other fruit)"; of "a forestall", and of instress, inscape, and inlaw. He uses almost a new language and doesn't provide a dictionary.

But there are marvellous passages—passages which we have seen in connection with his poems: such visions as the sight of the world in a drop of Christ's redeeming blood, of all things as "charged with God" so that "if we know how to touch them [they] give off sparks and take fire, yield drops and flow, ring and tell of him".[17]

There is a central thread running through these tentative notes and binding them together. This theme we have already seen in many of his poems and we shall see it expressed with new vigour and lucidity in the poem beginning "As kingfishers catch fire" (No. 34), written soon after he left his Tertianship: the individual reaches his highest perfection when, in co-operation with grace, he becomes another Christ. That is the motif of the Commentary, of his poems, and of his life. Hopkins emerged from his Tertianship with this ideal before him clearer than ever; and one cannot doubt that his whole spiritual life was deepened during this period when he was busy only with God, *vacans Deo.*

For the last seven years of his life, Hopkins' official duties were teaching and examining in the classics. His first appointment came upon the completion of his Tertianship when, in the fall of 1882, he became a member of the teaching staff at Stonyhurst College. There he taught Greek and Latin to candidates for the

degree examinations at the University of London. After a year
and a half he was elected, in January, 1884, to a fellowship at the
Royal University of Ireland.

"Ribblesdale" (1882), named after the Stonyhurst district in
Lancashire, is like such earlier poems as "Pied Beauty" and "Starlight Night" in its sacramental emphasis on the world as news of
God. But like "God's Grandeur", "In the Valley of the Elwy",
and "The Sea and the Skylark," in conclusion it puts its emphasis
on man, who does not correspond. The poem is spare and hard:

> Earth, sweet Earth, sweet landscape, with leavés throng
> And louchéd low grass,* heaven that dost appeal
> To, with no tongue to plead, no heart to feel;
> That canst but only be, but dost that long—
>
> Thou canst but be, but that thou well dost; strong
> Thy plea with him who dealt, nay does now deal,
> Thy lovely dale down thus and thus bids reel
> Thy river, and o'er gives all to rack or wrong.

One can see that, like many of the poems of 1877-9, this sonnet
draws on the notes (or the notes draw on the poem) which Hopkins
made on the introduction to the Spiritual Exercises which we
studied in relation to those earlier poems:

> "The sun and stars shining glorify God. . . . They glorify God,
> *but they do not know it* . . . they are something like him, they make
> him known . . . but they do not know they do. . . . Nevertheless
> what they can *they always do.*"

But in the last line of the octet we already have indicated to us
the contrast of man and his failure to fulfil his own purpose; for
man, we will recall, *"can mean to give him glory"*. Then comes
the question, "Does man then do it?" The sextet of "Ribblesdale"
sadly answers in the negative:

> And what is Earth's eye, tongue, or heart else, where
> Else, but in dear and dogged man?—Ah, the heir
> To his own selfbent so bound, so tied to his turn,
> To thriftless reave† both our rich round world bare
> And none reck of world after, this bids wear
> Earth brows of such care, care and dear concern.

* See Bridges' note: "In the letter to R.W.D. he writes: '*Louched* is a coinage
of mine, and is to mean much the same as slouched, slouching, and I mean
throng for an adjective as we use it in Lancashire'. But *louch* has ample authority, see the 'English Dialect Dictionary'."
† Rob, plunder, despoil.

Man has failed to co-operate with grace, refused to share the life of Christ. It is not surprising that when spring came to Stonyhurst in 1883, Hopkins should write a poem on the Blessed Virgin as the mediatrix of grace, for in his Commentary on the Exercises he had emphasized once more the importance of grace in man's life, in the supernatural life which is the life of grace. And his devotion to Mary, which has its roots in the Exercises, runs through his Jesuit life from "The Wreck of the Deutschland" onwards.

There is, it is true, something unsatisfactory about his Marian poems. And this is accounted for in large measure by the fact that they were, as he admitted, occasional pieces in which he especially wanted to appeal to popular taste. All of them—"The May Magnificat", "Ad Mariam" (if this is by the poet), "Rosa Mystica", "Ad Matrem Virginem", and "The Blessed Virgin compared to the Air we Breathe"—were written to be hung before the Lady Statue at Stonyhurst, where it was a custom in the month of May so to honour the Blessed Virgin.

But of these poems, "The Blessed Virgin compared to the Air we Breathe" is the most characteristic of Hopkins himself. It consists of one hundred and twenty-six delicately woven lines of extended metaphor: the air upon which our natural life is dependent is analogous to the Blessed Virgin as the mother of grace, the sustainer of our supernatural life.

It is the inexhaustible fecundity of Mary the Mediatrix of Grace that is the subject of the poem. Mary

> mothers each new grace
> That does now reach our race.

The climax is reached in a passage of great depth: the influx of grace within us is the birth of Christ within man, a re-incarnation of the Incarnation:

> Laying, like air's fine flood,
> The deathdance in his blood;
> Yet no part but what will
> Be Christ our Saviour still.
> Of her flesh he took flesh:
> He does take fresh and fresh,
> Though much the mystery how,
> Not flesh but spirit now
> And makes, O marvellous!
> New Nazareths in us.

Then comes a passage suggested by the following unpublished notes that Hopkins made for a sermon he preached four years earlier: "St. Bernard's saying, All grace is given through Mary: this is a mystery. Like blue sky, which for all its richness of colour does not stain the sunlight, though smoke and red clouds do, so God's graces comes to us unchanged but all through her."[19]

The poems ends with a tender prayer which felicitously brings to a close the metaphor which he has sustained for more than a hundred lines:

> Be thou then, O thou dear
> Mother, my atmosphere.

The fullness of the implications of the Commentary on the Exercises was to find poetical expression when Hopkins was at Stonyhurst. Shortly after he left his Tertianship he wrote an untitled poem which draws upon the thoughts he had crystallized during that period, when he had devoted himself so whole-heartedly to the spiritual life.

He had opened his Commentary with a consideration which he had long felt: the sharp individuality or "selfbent" which he found in all things, the beautiful uniqueness of the inscapes about him. He proceeded to express in a dozen different ways the distinctiveness of self; and human nature he found "more highly pitched, selved, and distinctive than anything in the world" And he concluded:

> Nothing else in nature comes near this unspeakable stress of pitch, distinctiveness, and selving, this selfbeing of my own. Nothing explains it or resembles it, except so far as this, that other men to themselves have the same feeling . . . searching nature I taste *self* but at one tankard, that of my own being.[20]

And now in his poem he finds each thing expressing its selfhood:

> As kingfishers catch fire, dragonflies dráw fláme;
> As tumbled over rim in roundy wells
> Stones ring; like each tucked string tells, each hung bell's
> Bow swung finds tongue to fling out broad its name;
> Each mortal thing does one thing and the same:
> Deals out that being indoors each one dwells;
> Selves—goes itself; *myself* it speaks and spells,
> Crying *Whát I do is me: for that I came.*

Then in the Commentary, as in the poem, Hopkins adds, "I say more". For he goes on to say that the most sharply differentiated of all things, man, is perfected by the exercise of that selfhood which is the will. And the highest development, the most expressive expressiveness of that "I or me" is when man freely co-operates with grace and becomes an *alter Christus*. "Unumquodque tendens in suam perfectionem tendit in divinam similitudinem", said St. Thomas; and Hopkins maintained the same: each thing striving after its own perfection strives to attain the likeness of the divine. Man becomes Christ through correspondence with grace, the life of Christ within him; "so far as it is action, correspondence, on the creature's [part] it is *actio salutaris*; so far as it is looked at *in esse quieto* it is Christ in his member on the one side, his member in Christ on the other". And Hopkins adds a further passage which is an exegesis of the closing lines of the poem: "It is as if a man said: That is Christ playing at me and me playing at Christ, only that it is no play but truth; That is Christ *being me* and me being Christ:"[21]

> I say móre: the just man justices;
> Kéeps gráce: thát keeps all his goings graces;
> Acts in God's eye what in God's eye he is—
> Chríst—for Christ plays in ten thousand places,
> Lovely in limbs, and lovely in eyes not his
> To the Father through the features of men's faces.

This transubstantiation takes place when, in Hopkins' words, "the member is in all things conformed to Christ".

And this is not the annihilation of selfhood, he continues, but fulfilment: "This too best brings out the nature of the man himself, as the lettering on a sail or device upon a flag are best seen when it fills."[22] Thus it is that he can say: "It is the holiest that shews his freedom most."[23]

Dublin and Desolation

MUCH of the misunderstanding which has surrounded Hopkins is a misunderstanding of the last years of his life when he was in Dublin. Certain difficulties which have been very minor now become important and acute. New problems arise. In spite of the scanty materials at our disposal and in spite of the complexity of interaction between the many elements which were making his life, the general pattern of Hopkins' last five years is clear.

It was in January, 1884, that Hopkins was elected to a fellowship at the Royal University of Ireland, as it was then called. One of his contemporaries in the Society of Jesus has related part of the story of his election:

> I have heard from Lord Emly, the Vice-Chancellor of the University, that the recommendatory letters presented when he sought election, spoke so highly of his character and attainments (especially one from Dr. Jowett, the Master of Balliol, in praise of his scholarship), as to make the Senate most anxious to obtain his services.[1]

The Royal University of Ireland was only an examining and degree-giving university, modelled on the plan of London. Associated with it was University College, which during the 'eighties was run by the Jesuits, so that Hopkins held a fellowship in the Royal University and at the same time was on the faculty of University College.

The whole foundation had had its origin in Newman's efforts to establish a "Catholic Oxford" in Dublin, but after his leaving Ireland and subsequent resignation from the rectorship in 1858 the University had an existence more vacillating then ever. University College, a product of an effort at reorganization in the early 'eighties, was one of the many attempts to bring vitality to the Royal University. The College performed useful service, but its continuance was constantly endangered by lack of funds or by plans for a new and further reorganization. The uncertainty of its career is reflected in numerous letters that Hopkins wrote while he was there; for instance, he wrote to Newman:

This poor University College, the somehow-or-other-manned wreck of the Catholic University is afloat and not sinking; rather making a very little way than losing any. There is scarcely any public interest in the University question. Nay. there is none. But this does not prevent good and really patriotic people in a quiet, but not ineffective way, doing what can be done to advance it.[3]

The staff which Hopkins joined at St. Patrick's House, Stephen's Green, was apparently competent and earnest, though there may be slight exaggeration or unconscious satire in Dom Wulstan Phillipson's statement that "Father Hopkins lived in Dublin with men who might be found among the dons of any of the Oxford or Cambridge Colleges of the time". Some of the laymen—John Casey, Robert Ornsby, and Thomas Arnold, son of Arnold of Rugby—had formed the nucleus of Newman's staff more than twenty-five years before. But new blood had been added during the reorganization and several excellent Jesuits—such men as Father William Delaney, its President, and Father Joseph Darlington, its Dean of Studies—were devoting themselves to the success of the College.

Hopkins' official duties involved not only the teaching of Greek and Latin in University College, but also the preparing and grading of examinations for degrees given by the Royal University. Registration at the college was about two hundred students during these years; Hopkins' classes are said to have been small.

He left Stonyhurst for his Fellowship in poor health and with the feeling that he was not properly prepared for the work he was to do. His attitude may be seen in two letters he wrote soon after he had entered upon his new responsibilities. The first was to Newman, sent off almost as soon as he landed in Dublin. "I am writing", he told his old friend who had himself laboured at the Irish university,

> from where I never thought to be, in a University for Catholic Ireland begun under your leadership, which has since those days indeed long and unhappily languished, but for which we now—with God's help—hope a continuation or restoration of success. In the events which have brought me here I recognize the hand of providence, but nevertheless have felt and feel an unfitness which led me at first to try to decline the offer made me and now does not allow my spirits to rise to the level of the position and its duties.

Characteristically, his faith rebukes him, and he adds, "But perhaps the things of most promise with God begin with weakness and fear".[3] It was not so much that he felt unprepared for the Latin and Greek, though in everything he held before himself the most exacting standards of perfection, but he faced Dublin in ill health. In a letter informing Bridges of his new station, he wrote:

> It is an honour and an opening and has many bright sides, but at present it has also some dark ones and this in particular that I am not at all strong, not strong enough for the requirements, and do not see at all how I am to become so.

Dublin itself he found as uncongenial as Bedford Leigh or Liverpool; he notes:

> I have been warmly welcomed and most kindly treated. But Dublin itself is a joyless place and I think in my heart as smoky as London is: I had fancied it quite different. The Phoenix Park is fine, but inconveniently far off.

While he apparently enjoyed his teaching, he very much disliked the drudgery of his duties as examiner. In his very first Irish letter to Bridges he told how the anticipation of these duties in his weak state of health did not make him look forward to life in Dublin:

> When I first contemplated the six examinations I have yearly to conduct, five of them running, and to the Matriculation there came up last year 750 candidates, I thought that Stephen's Green (the biggest square in Europe) paved with gold would not pay for it.[4]

His conscientiousness made the awarding of marks a momentous matter. No one who reads his Dublin letters can doubt for a moment that he found his work as examiner genuinely torturing; his weak health and especially the troublesome state of his eyes served to accentuate his difficulties. For five years he applied himself to the heavy duties of marking numerous examinations. How hard he found this task is shown in a letter to Bridges a half-year after his arrival in Dublin; he tells his friend not to send one of his poems for comment:

> I am in the very thick of examination work and in danger of permanently injuring my eyes. I shall have no time at all till past the middle of next month and not much then, for I have to begin lecturing and cannot now prepare.[5]

Subsequent remarks about his work as examiner range from a short statement of facts like, "A consignment of 331 examination papers to-night, I [am sorry] to say, and more will come", to confessions of weariness like, "I have just begun my examining and shall be hard at it for weeks, a weary task indeed". Sometimes he can be almost amusing about it, as when he tells Canon Dixon that one of his pieces of music had not been sung: "If it had been I could not have heard it, for I was helping to save and damn the studious youth of Ireland." In still another letter he admits, "It is killing work to examine a nation". These remarks may seem flippant out of their context, but Hopkins was in earnest.[6] After a summer vacation in Wales succeeded by the fall examinations, he wrote to Bridges:

> My examinations are over till the next attack of the plague. . . . I was I cannot tell when in such health and spirits as on my return from Cadwalader and all his goats but 331 accounts of the First Punic War with trimmings, have sweated me down to nearer my lees and usual alluvial low water mudflats, groans, despair, and yearnings.[7]

Less than a year before he died he summarized his work as Fellow of the Royal University: "This morning I gave in what I believe is the last batch of examination-work for this autumn (and if all were seen, fallen leaves of my poor life between all the leaves of it)."[8]

To what extent the burdensomeness of his duties was conditioned by his health, or how far his routine influenced his health, we can hardly determine on the basis of his letters. Seemingly his physiological state and his mental outlook interacted to produce a complex condition to which each contributed, though we cannot determine the exact share of each. Undoubtedly a weak body made difficult certain problems which would otherwise have been more easily solved; discouragements and heavy duties may have accentuated and sharpened his bodily suffering.

We know that as a youth he was delicate and pale. The degree of his sensitivity is indicated in a remarkable passage in the Journal he kept as a novice and scholastic; after a passage of gorgeous description setting down the beauties of sky and sea which he had seen during a vacation in August, 1873, he had entered:

> But we hurried too fast and it knocked me up. We went to the

College, the seminary being wanted for the secular priests' retreat: almost no gas, for the retorts are being mended; therefore candles in bottles, things not ready, darkness and despair. In fact being unwell I was quite downcast: nature in all her parcels and faculties gaped and fell apart, *fatiscebat*, like a clod cleaving and holding only by strings of root.[9]

With a sensibility so sharply responsive to ill health and physical hardships, he lived his life until he died of a contagious fever in 1889. To see how powerfully a physiological state could affect his mental attitude and even his view of nature, makes it easier for us to appreciate some of the sufferings he endured in his later years. And it is to be realized that this sensitivity is a part of his poetry. Nothing could be more unfair or untruthful than to attribute all his sufferings to his membership of the Society of Jesus. His sensitivity and his high-strung temperament in part predestined him to suffering. Even six months before he entered the novitiate he had written to Baillie from the Oratory School, to which he went as a master after he left Balliol:

> I must say that I am very anxious to get away from this place. I have become very weak in health and do not seem to recover myself here or likely to do so. Teaching is very burdensome, especially when you have much of it: I have. I have not much time and almost no energy—for I am always tired—to do anything on my own account.[10]

An operation which he underwent as a young man of twenty-eight seems, on the evidence of his note-books and letters, to have left him easily subject to fatigue. Seven years after it, in a letter to Bridges, himself a doctor, Hopkins explains that his own physician had traced his nervous fatigue to an irritation left by this operation. How depressed was his view of life when he was unwell is clear from letters he wrote to Bridges from Chesterfield in 1878 and from Liverpool in 1880. In the first he says:

> Write me an interesting letter. I cannot do so. Life here is as dank as ditch-water and has some of the other qualities of ditch-water: at least I know that I am reduced to great weakness by diarrhoea, which lasts too, as if I were poisoned.[11]

In that letter we have, too, that feeling of impotence, of inability to produce even a letter. "I take up a languid pen to write to you", he complained from Liverpool, "being down with diarrhoea and vomiting, brought on by yesterday's heat and the long hours in the confessional."[12]

In his letter to Bridges announcing his election as Fellow of the Royal University he had pointed to his lack of strength as making him reluctant to accept the heavy duties which his new appointment would entail. His health definitely declined in Dublin and everything seemed to go wrong in his world of nervous prostration. In 1884-5 he seems to have reached his lowest ebb, and such phrases as "that coffin of weakness and dejection in which I live" are not infrequent.[13]

To his lifelong friend Baillie he wrote:

> The melancholy I have all my life been subject to has become of late years not indeed more intense in its fits but rather more distributed, constant, and crippling. One, the lightest but a very inconvenient form of it, is daily anxiety about work to be done, which makes me break off or never finish all that lies outside that work. It is useless to write more on this: when I am at the worst, though my judgment is never affected, my state is much like madness. I see no ground for thinking I shall ever get over it or ever succeed in doing anything that is not forced on me to do of any consequence.[14]

Hopkins' own most frequent prescription for himself is change. One of his Jesuit contemporaries who knew him well during his Dublin years has noted a scrupulosity in his attitude towards asking for permission to arrange any changes in his routine:

> During the few years of which I speak [the Dublin years], he was very seldom away from home, having a notion that he ought not to take a holiday unless his health required it. . . . He was of a very retiring disposition and made few acquaintances in Dublin, even these he seldom visited, and very rarely could he be induced to ask permission to lunch or dine out.[15]

At times there is a very thin line between Hopkins' conscientious effort to live the Exercises and practise the Rules of the Society and a certain strain of scrupulosity which had manifested itself even in his Oxford days. Anyone who knows the Exercises must be impressed with St. Ignatius' efforts to guard against any energy-paralyzing scrupulosity. Father D'Arcy has admirably indicated the root of Hopkins' difficulty:

> In all this he is literal-minded and refuses to distinguish between the serious and the light or fantastic, duty and that happy

love which enables the children of God to act in full liberty of spirit. Quite possibly the fact that he was a convert and that he had been brought up in the atmosphere of rectitude wl.ich belongs so especially to Victorian religion, may help to account for some of the puzzles of his character. He was in sentiment and by education a thorough Victorian, and it was through this habit of mind a genius quite un-Victorian had to work. Other converts have exhibited the same unresolved tension. They have startled, and still startle the traditional Catholic by their inability to unbend.[16]

Hopkins seems to have realized that the responsibility was with him to ask for the necessary changes, for in 1885—the year he was suffering very deeply from his nervous fatigue and weakness—he noted, after a vacation in England:

> Now because I have had a holiday though not strong I have some buoyancy; soon I am afraid I shall be ground down to a state like this last spring's and summer's, . . . and nobody was to blame, except myself partly for not managing myself better and contriving a change.[17]

If one looks objectively at the chronology of these years in Dublin, one is inclined to conclude that Hopkins had a fair number of vacations and holidays: several times he took a holiday at Clongowes-Wood College; one Christmas was spent with Lord Emly; others with his friends, the Cassidys of Monastereven; at least once he went to the country home of Judge O'Hagan at Glenaveena; he made a trip through Galway and Clare one spring; he even took some of his vacations outside of Ireland, for in August, 1885, he went to England; the next summer he was in England and Wales; during the summer of 1887 he went to see Bridges and Patmore; the next August he went to Fort William in Scotland.

Objectively, I say, one would think that Hopkins had his share of change. But in his complicated state of physical weakness and mental depression, change proved to be of little relief. How this could be true is hinted in a letter which he wrote to Bridges almost immediately after his return to Dublin from a vacation in England:

> Though you have a good deal of pleasing modern author to comment on I add a postscript more. You must have been surprised at his saying on his return from a 3-weeks' holiday that he could get no relief and so on. But what he wishes to be understood

is that his work, which is so harassing to his mind, was only suspended for that time (which of itself was most helpful and quite necessary) and not for the time finished and done; so that there is no end to anxiety and care, but only an interruption of it, and the effect accumulates on the whole.[18]

For his last two years in Dublin (1887-9) Hopkins' trouble with his eyes became more acute: "The eyes are almost out of my head . . . to bed, to bed; my eyes are almost bleeding . . . the feeling is like soap or lemons."[19]

But perhaps the most incisive statement of his condition and its effect on him as teacher, examiner, priest, and poet is stated in his words: "I only need one thing—a working health, a working strength; with that, any employment is tolerable or pleasant, enough for human nature; without it, things are liable to go very hardly with it."[20]

But ill health with its complex train of mental sufferings and the drudgery and routine of examining were not the only difficulties of Hopkins in Dublin. Among others was his strong attachment to England and his disapproval of the Irish political movements of the 'eighties. While we must not think of his political interests as being one of his heaviest crosses, yet they did form a very real part of his outlook.

Hopkins was in many ways a very English Englishman. His patriotism and devotion to England were apparent long before he took up residence in Dublin—recall, for instance, the close of "The Wreck of the Deutschland". The Dublin of the 1880's would have been a difficult place for any patriotic Englishman. It was the decade of Parnell's ascendancy, and his objective was, in the words of Stephen Gwynn, "to destroy the monopoly of power possessed by those who called themselves 'England's faithful garrison'." Not only was agrarian agitation almost at its revolutionary height, but the movement for Home Rule was gaining strength. Further, to make the situation more difficult for Hopkins, the Royal University was nationalist in its objectives; to make matters more acute for him, some of the Catholic bishops, especially Archbishop Walsh of Dublin and Archbishop Croke of Cashel, identified themselves with the nationalist cause.

It was with approval, then, that the English Jesuit welcomed the Papal Rescript condemning the Plan of the Campaign which Parnell had directed at the English landlords. To Newman he wrote:

Politically, the times are most troubled. I live, I may say, in an air most painful to breathe and this comes home to me more, not less, with time. There is to my mind only one break in the sky, but it is a notable one; it is from Rome. The Pope is acting very much as I thought he would and the effect of what he does, though slowly and guardedly, is likely to be powerful.[21]

The extent to which Hopkins disapproved of the nationalist spirit which permeated the Ireland of his day is illustrated by a story which has been told about him. When the Royal University was conferring degrees one year, the audience sang a nationalist song. Hopkins rose and left. The next day he confided to a Jesuit friend, "You know, I would not have done that if it hadn't been so wicked!"

He never came to understand the Irish even to the extent that Newman did. To one of Hopkins' letters which does not survive, Newman replied:

Your letter is an appalling one—but not on that account untrustworthy. There is one consideration however which you omit. The Irish Patriots hold that they never have yielded themselves to the sway of England and therefore have never been under her laws, and have never been rebels.

This does not diminish the force of your picture, but it suggests that there is no help, no remedy. If I were an Irishman, I should be (in heart) a rebel. Moreover, to clench the difficulty the Irish character and tastes [are] very different from the English.[22]

The effect of the Irish political situation on Hopkins seems merely to have intensified his own devotion to England. His attitude towards poetry was always patriotic, for he considered that poetry itself contributed powerfully to a national culture. In poems he wrote during his years in Dublin he referred to "England, whose honour O all my heart woos" and he advised:

Call me England's fame's fond lover,
Her fame to keep, her fame to recover.

In two letters he makes his position clear. "Your poems", he told Patmore,

are a good deed done for the Catholic Church and another for England, for the British Empire. . . . What marked and striking excellence has England to shew to make her civilisation attractive? Her literature is one of her excellences and attractions and I believe that criticism will tend to make this more and more felt;

but there must be more of that literature, a continued supply and in quality excellent. This is why I hold that fine works of art, and especially if, like yours, that are not only ideal in form but deal with high matter as well, are really a great power in the world, an element of strength even to an empire.[23]

He wrote a letter not unlike this to Canon Dixon; and to Bridges he said:

A great work by an Englishman is like a great battle won by England. It is an unfading bay tree. It will even be admired by and praised by and do good to those who hate England (as England is most perilously hated), who do not wish even to be benefited by her. It is then even a patriotic duty $\tau\hat{\eta}$ $\pi o\iota\acute{\eta}\sigma\epsilon\iota$ $\acute{\epsilon}\nu\epsilon\rho\gamma\epsilon\hat{\iota}\nu$ and to secure the fame and permanence of the work.[24]

These were Hopkins' letters to his friends and they introduce us to a further difficulty which Hopkins experienced in Dublin: he himself found it almost impossible to produce poetry or anything else. In order to understand his condition we must go back to the time that he entered the Society of Jesus, to sketch the problems of one who was at the same time a poet and a Jesuit.

To begin with, Hopkins had not consecrated himself to the Society in order to give himself an opportunity to be a poet— even a religious or devotional poet. He joined the sons of Ignatius fully aware of the sacrifice which dedication to the religious life would demand. He realized that his opportunities would be circumscribed and that he might be assigned to stations and duties which would entirely preclude the production of poetry. Some six months before he entered the Jesuit novitiate at Roehampton— indeed two months before he decided that he would become a Jesuit rather than a Benedictine or a secular priest—he had written to Baillie: "I want to write still and as a priest I very likely can do that too, not so freely as I shd. have liked, e.g. nothing or little in the verse way, but no doubt what wd. best serve the cause of my religion."[25] He wanted his whole life and activity to contribute as directly as possible to the goal he was about to choose. Then as the time approached for his entrance into the Society of Jesus he decided to destroy anything which might come between himself and his fullest dedication to the religious life; he voluntarily made a holocaust of his poetry; as a sacrifice to God he destroyed his verses so that he might join His servants without any barriers, without any personal predilections and attachments. If his superiors, for him the representatives of Christ, should suggest that he write poetry, then he would be free to dedicate his powers as a poet to God. But he wanted to enter the novitiate with nothing standing between him and God. "I cannot send my *Summa*", he wrote to Bridges that August, "for it is burnt with my other verses: I saw they wd. interfere with my state and vocation."[26]

We have already seen how he came to break his poetic silence; but every sentence here is important. If we are to understand what so often has been misunderstood, we must look once more at his words to Canon Dixon, who had asked him in one of his first letters whether he wrote poetry. "You ask", replied Hopkins,

> Do I write verse myself? What I had written I burnt before I became a Jesuit and resolved to write no more, as not belonging to my profession, unless it were by the wish of my superiors; so for seven years I wrote nothing but two or three little presentation pieces which occasion called for. But when in the winter of '75 the Deutschland was wrecked... I was affected by the account and happening to say so to my rector he said that he wished someone would write a poem on the subject. On this hint I set to work and, though my hand was out at first, produced one.... After writing this I held myself free to compose, but cannot find it in my conscience to spend time upon it; so I have done little and shall do less.[27]

God, through his superiors, had lifted the ban. Yes. But was it not that he himself had desired his own will in this, and that God had merely treated him as a pining child? He would never know, quite, what was the answer to this question. It would trouble him to the end, and humble him, and chasten him too. It would make him cling to one last silence—the desire to avoid publication, to sing because he must, but to confide his songs to few ears, to be chary of fame, to need, in the necessity of communication, an audience, and to deny himself all but the most limited of audiences, and those only who could not fully understand him. This was his sacrifice. It limited his output, but it sharpened the steel of his verse. It made him less prolific; but it robbed him of no power.

After telling how this self-imposed ban had been lifted and how he therefore felt free once more to write poetry, he wrote a very important sentence—one that is to echo in his Dublin period: "But even the impulse to write is wanting, for I have no thought of publishing."[28] This was the sacrifice he made, the sacrifice of fame, of recognition, of acclaim. And it was a hard sacrifice for this artist. But he left this in the hands of God, and God, he thought, asked this sacrifice of him for the rest of his life.

Thus Hopkins left any movement towards publication to his superiors. He admitted: "I could wish, I allow, that my pieces could at some time become known but in some spontaneous way, so to speak, and without my forcing."[29] But this desire was qualified even further: "If some one in authority knew of my having some poems printable and suggested my doing it I shd. not refuse, I should be partly, though not altogether, glad."[30]

In order to understand this rather complex attitude we may turn to the Spiritual Exercises. In the "Principle and Foundation" indifference to applause and recognition is laid down as a prerequisite to the spiritual life. "It is necessary", wrote St. Ignatius,

> to make ourselves indifferent to all that is allowed to the choice of our free will and is not prohibited to it; so that, on our part, we want not . . . honour rather than dishonour . . . desiring and choosing only what is most conducive for us to the end for which we are created.

But Ignatian spirituality—and in this it is often misunderstood—goes far beyond this mere indifference or detachment, for these are merely the attitudes of mind necessary so that in the rest of the Exercises the Jesuit may seek out the positive will of God. Indeed if he is called to imitate Christ he will choose obscurity, "contumely or contempt", rather than "worldly honour". The most perfect humility is one in which,

> In order to imitate and be more actually like Christ Our Lord, I want and choose poverty with Christ poor rather than riches, opprobrium with Christ replete with it rather than honours; and to desire to be rated as worthless and a fool for Christ, Who first was held such, rather than wise or prudent in this world.

And having chosen to follow Christ rather than the world, Hopkins chose obscurity. This does not mean that there was no pain involved, but it was often the pain of love, a pain which transfigures. Hopkins was indeed an anxious soul.

As an artist he knew that publication is yearned for: " 'Fame is the spur that the clear spirit doth raise To shun delights and live laborious days'—a spur very hard to find a substitute for or to do without."[31] But at the same time as a religious, as one who was attempting to be another Christ, he saw fame as "a great danger in itself, as dangerous as wealth every bit, I should think, and as hard to enter the kingdom of heaven with."[32]

In the long letter to Canon Dixon it will be noted further that Hopkins says, "I . . . cannot find it in my conscience to spend time upon it".[33] Indeed in one of his letters he goes even further: "It always seems to me that poetry is unprofessional," and he adds, "but that is what I have said to myself, not others to me."[34] For Hopkins first duties always came first, and a number of duties came before poetry. First of all came his own personal sanctification and perfection. He constantly endeavoured to fulfil the exhortation which the founder of the Jesuits had laid down as a rule for his followers: "All those who have joined the Society must devote themselves to the study of solid and perfect virtues and spiritual things and regard these as more important than learning or other natural human gifts." (Rule 16) He had, first of all, to try to live the Spiritual Exercises. "If we care for fine verses", he said to Bridges, "how much more for a noble life."[35]

Next came the specific "professional" duties of the particular station to which he was assigned by his superiors. And his Order never created an office of poet laureate for him to fill.

It may seem harsh of Hopkins to think of his verse as "unprofessional", for we have seen how deeply religious was his poetry, how it might in fact be considered as a hymn of praise to God, how St. Ignatius himself had said that "if everything is directed towards God, everything is prayer". Indeed Hopkins had written, in one of the most delightful prose passages he ever produced:

> When a man is in God's grace and free from mortal sin, then everything he does, so long as there is no sin in it, gives God glory and what does not give him glory has some, however little, sin in it. It is not only prayer that gives God glory but work. Smiting an anvil, sawing a beam, whitewashing a wall, driving horses, sweeping, scouring, everything gives God some glory if being in his grace you do it as your duty. To go to communion worthily gives God great glory, but to take food in thankfulness and temperance gives him glory too. To lift up the hands in prayer gives God glory, but a man with a dungfork in his hand, a woman with a slop-pail, give him glory too. He is so great that all things give him glory if you mean they should. So then, my brethren, live.[36]

According to this view poetry, and more especially religious poetry may give God glory. How then could Hopkins say that his own devotional poetry was unprofessional? Unless we realize how for him the duties of priesthood took precedence over all things we shall hopelessly misinterpret his attitude. In the above passage he says, "Everything gives God glory if being in his grace you do it as your duty"—and for Hopkins the duties of his state of life, full of difficult and harassing problems, were all-important. Beside them the gift for poetry, even fired as it was with a deeply religious attitude, was almost nothing. His consecration to the priesthood was complete and final. No wonder, then, that he considered his poetry secondary to his own perfection and the perfection of his neighbour. That his poems are instruments of praise one cannot doubt. But Hopkins himself never doubted that his functions as a priest praised God even more.

We will recall how heavy Hopkins found the duties of parish work, what a "slavery of mind" he found living in the dismal confines of Liverpool or Bedford Leigh, how the contact with sordidness and sin saddened and depressed him, how his body was broken and life a burden. His consecration to the priesthood brought him these things. Indeed he summed up this period of his active ministry prior to his Tertianship when he wrote, "The parish work of Liverpool is wearying to mind and body and leaves me nothing but odds and ends of time. There is merit in it but little Muse".[37] But we know how incomparably greater to Hopkins was the priesthood than "muse of mounting vein".

The poet's second period of "elected silence" came during his Tertianship, when he reviewed his own life in the Society of Jesus and rededicated himself to the ideals of St. Ignatius. It was during that period that he wrote to Canon Dixon two long but very important letters which review and summarize his attitude to his art and to his priesthood. They say almost all that can be said. "I am ashamed at the expressions of high regard which your last letter and others have contained, kind and touching as they are, and do not know whether I ought to reply to them or not," but Hopkins goes on to state at length his attitude:

> This I say: my vocation puts before me a standard so high that a higher can be found nowhere else. The question then for me is not whether I am willing (if I may guess what is in your mind) to make a sacrifice of hopes of fame (let us suppose), but whether I am not to undergo a severe judgment from God for the lothness I have shewn in making it, for the reserves I may have in my heart

made, for the backward glances I have given with my hand upon
the plough, for the waste of time the very compositions you admire
may have caused and their preoccupation of the mind which be-
longed to more sacred or more binding duties, for the disquiet
and the thoughts of vainglory they have given rise to. A purpose
may look smooth and perfect from without but be frayed and
faltering from within.... I destroyed the verse I had written
when I entered the Society and meant to write no more; the
Deutschland I began after a long interval at the chance suggestion
of my superior, but that being done it is a question whether I did
well to write anything else. However I shall, in my present mind,
continue to compose, as occasion shall fairly allow, which I am
afraid will be seldom and indeed for some years past has been
scarcely ever, and let what I produce wait and take its chance; for
a very spiritual man once told me that with things like composition
the best sacrifice was not to destroy one's work but to leave it
entirely to be disposed of by obedience. But I can scarcely fancy
myself asking a superior to publish a volume of my verses and I
own that humanly there is very little likelihood of that ever coming
to pass. And to be sure if I chose to look at things on one side
and not the other I could of course regret this bitterly. But there
is more peace and it is the holier lot to be unknown than to be
known.[38]

In his reply Canon Dixon touched what many after him have
seen as one of the most central difficulties in the study of Hopkins'
life, for he remarked: "Surely one vocation cannot destroy another."[39] But it is not so much a matter of "destruction". For a
Jesuit priest, Christ's service is more important than Muse. This
does not mean that the Muse—if she is pure—is to be damned as a
harlot. But it does mean that she will take a second or third or
even tenth place. It may mean that she might have to be sacrificed
completely. But there is a vast difference between sacrifice and
destruction, which Hopkins knew but which the world often knows
not. And the fullness of his devotion to the spiritual life is magni-
ficently epitomized in his letter of reply:

When a man has given himself to God's service, when he has
denied himself and followed Christ, he has fitted himself to receive
and does receive from God a special guidance, a more particular
providence. This guidance is conveyed partly by the action of
other men, as his appointed superiors, and partly by direct lights
and inspirations. If I wait for such guidance, through whatever
channel conveyed, about anything, about my poetry for instance,

I do more wisely in every way than if I try to serve my own seeming interests in the matter. Now if you value what I write, if I do myself, much more does our Lord. And if he chooses to avail himself of what I leave at his disposal he can do so with a felicity and with a success which I could never command. And if he does not, then two things follow; one that the reward I shall nevertheless receive from him will be all the greater; the other that then I shall know how much a thing contrary to his will and even to my own best interests I should have done if I had taken things into my own hands and forced on publication. This is my principle and this in the main has been my practice: leading the sort of life I do here it seems easy, but when one mixes with the world and meets on every side its secret solicitations, to live by faith is harder, is very hard; nevertheless by God's help I shall always do so.[40]

Thus did Hopkins resolve to waive publication and recognition as long as God seemed to wish that sacrifice. Canon Dixon had expressed the hope that Hopkins might "be sanctioned and encouraged by the great Society to which you belong, which has given so many ornaments to literature".[41] But Hopkins realized that the duties of his state of life were other than the writing of verses, that heroic sanctity—for Hopkins was aiming at that—alone can compensate for the fame that genius attracts, that it was "the holier lot to be unknown". Thus he writes in the same letter:

> Our Society values, as you say, and has contributed to literature, to culture; but only as a means to an end. Its history and its experience shew that literature proper, as poetry, has seldom been found to be to that end a very serviceable means. We have had for three centuries often the flower of the youth of a country in numbers enter our body: among these how many poets, how many artists of all sorts, there must have been! But there have been very few Jesuit poets and, where they have been, I believe it would be found on examination that there was something exceptional in their circumstances or, so to say, counterbalancing in their career. For genius attracts fame and individual fame St. Ignatius looked on as the most dangerous and dazzling of all attractions.[42]

Then he reviews the cases of numerous Jesuit poets, artists, orators, philosophers, and saints. Of the poets he says,

> In England we had Fr. Southwell a poet, a minor poet but still a poet; but he wrote amidst a terrible persecution and died a martyr, with circumstances of horrible barbarity: this is the counterpoise in his career. Then what a genius was Campion himself!

was not he a poet? perhaps a great one, if he had chosen. . . . It seems in time he might have done anything. But-his eloquence died on the air, his genius was quenched in his blood after one year's employment in his country.[43]

And he sums up this whole section—showing how even St. Ignatius lived the hidden life—by saying, "I quote these cases to prove that show and brilliancy do not suit us, that we cultivate the commonplace outwardly and wish the beauty of the king's daughter, the soul, to be from within".[44]

Such, then, was the measure of Hopkins' dedication and sacrifice. And following his Tertianship his years in Dublin were to bring even greater sacrifice, and they were to bring great suffering.

In Dublin his ill health, with the mental fatigue, depression, and tedium which accompanied it, the routine of heavy duties amidst uncongenial surroundings, the strenuous effort to fulfil, at a time of great trial, the Ignatian ideals of perfection and sanctity—all these interacted and combined to make his "winter world".

He tried to complete his drama about St. Winefred, he tried to finish an ode on Campion, he tried to compose new poems—but he was dry.

He felt that his new position as Fellow at the Royal University demanded that he turn out papers dealing with classical antiquities. He had considered his Commentary on the Exercises "very professional"; probably for the same reason he now thought of editing a new critical edition of St. Patrick's "Confessions". His letters of 1884-9 are filled with dozens of projects, contemplated or started, ranging from short studies such as a "quasi-philosophical paper on the Greek Negatives" to a full-length book which was to deal chiefly with the art of the Greek lyric poets. For many years his interest in music had been increasing, and during his Dublin residence he turned to it more and more. His justifications for the time devoted to music may have been many, but at least one of them is suggested in a letter in which he remarks, "Music is more professional than poetry perhaps and Jesuits have composed and well, but none has any fame to speak of".[45]

But his attempts at poetry, music, and classical research came to almost nothing. "Unhappily", he wrote, "I cannot produce anything at all, not only the luxuries like poetry, but the duties almost of my position, its natural outcome—like scientific works".[46]

However many were the causes contributing to this general impotence—and they probably were many and various—one of the most important was his sacrifice of publication and fame. In 1886 he wrote a letter to Bridges which conveys the strength of his opinion that recognition is almost the necessary condition of art:

> By the bye, I say it deliberately and before. God, I would have you and Canon Dixon and all true poets remember that fame, the being known, though in itself one of the most dangerous things to man, is nevertheless the true [he had written "necessary" and then cancelled it] and appointed air, element, and setting of genius and its works. . . . We must then try to be known, aim at it, take means to it.

Yet the conclusion to this same letter recognizes that for himself certain other things must be put above art and its recognition. "Art and its fame do not really matter", the priest continued,

> spiritually they are nothing, virtue is the only good; but it is only by bringing in the infinite that to a just judgment they can be made to look infinitesimal or small or less than vastly great; and in this ordinary view of them I apply to them, and it is the true rule for dealing with them, what Christ our Lord said of virtue, Let your light shine before men that they may see your good works (say, of art) and glorify yr. Father in heaven.[47]

But for himself he did "bring in the infinite" and his renunciation of fame was tantamount, in his opinion, to renouncing the very springs of art.

For a time he had found it possible to produce even without encouragement, but now in Dublin he sadly confesses to Bridges: "There is a point with me in matters of any size when I must absolutely have encouragement as much as crops rain; afterwards I am independent."[48] But even this small encouragement was lacking and gradually he lost all impulse to create. Then his cry from the depths of his impotence is even greater. Then he feels that even recognition means nothing, but the absence of any well-spring of art becomes torturing stagnation:

> The fine pleasure is not to do a thing but to feel that you could and the mortification that goes to the heart is to feel it is the power that fails you: *qui occidere nolunt Posse volunt*; it is the refusal of a thing that we like to have. So with me, if I could but get on, if I could but produce work I should not mind its being buried, silenced, and going no further; but it kills me to be time's eunuch and never to beget.[49]

Such were his words in 1885; three years later, a year before his death, his anguished cry is the same, but the terms in which he expresses it suggest a more definitely spiritual implication: "All impulse fails me: I can give myself no sufficient reason for going on. Nothing comes: I am a eunuch—but it is for the kingdom of heaven's sake."[50] Here we have his recognition that his suffering, his impotence, his aridity was a sacrifice, that he was one of those described in St. Matthew: "And there are eunuchs, who have made themselves eunuchs for the kingdom of heaven."

Obviously the only way of judging adequately this priest who was also a poet is by "bringing in the infinite", the *primauté du spirituel*—the standard by which he judged himself and wanted to be judged. It is on the spiritual plane of sacrifice and of love that we must evaluate Hopkins. He knew so well that the very essence of perfection is the love of God unto the immolation of self, and he prayed in the final section of the Exercises,

> Take, Lord, and receive all my liberty, my memory, my intellect, and all my will—all that I have and possess. Thou gavest it to me: to Thee, Lord, I return it! All is Thine, dispose of it according to all Thy will.

When, during his Tertianship, he came to comment on this section he saw it as a love-sacrifice: "Here everything is of love, the love and duty of a grateful friend—and it serves as a foundation for the rest of life."[51] And that is the life that Hopkins lived.

To judge Hopkins by other standards is always to go astray. So when Claude Colleer Abbott writes that "he lacked, so it seems to me, just that serene certainty of how to serve God", he fails to see that it was to a life of sacrifice that Hopkins had dedicated himself. "And this conduct", said Christ to Marie Lataste, a spiritual writer to whom the priest was especially devoted during the last years of his life, "the world calls folly. It is folly, in fact; the folly of my Cross, the folly of my Cross which humbles, the folly of My Cross which forgives, the folly of My Cross which embraces all men, the folly of My Cross which unites to God. This folly is true wisdom".

How thoroughly Hopkins believed and tried to follow the Cross is clear throughout his poems and letters:

> O then, weary then why should we tread? O why are we so haggard
> at the heart, so care-coiled, care-killed, so fagged, so fashed, so
> cogged, so cumbered.

And to spiritual eyes there is a beauty far greater than mere physical beauty, flashed off by his devotion to the ideal, when "strung by duty" he himself is "strained to beauty" and

> the fire that breaks from thee then, a billion
> Times told lovelier, more dangerous, O my chevalier!

Thus Hopkins himself is always introducing the criterion by which he is to be judged: he wanted his life to be seen through Christ's eyes, and he looked not to the world but to Christ as the ultimate critic of all he did and thought: "The only just judge, the only just literary critic, is Christ, who prizes, is proud of, and admires, more than any man, more than the receiver himself can, the gifts of his own making."[52]

And Christ was not to leave his sacrifice entirely unrewarded even in this world. In the stagnation of the poet's greatest aridity —during the year 1885—He sent the sonnets, probably Hopkins' greatest poetry, which came, as the poet says, "unbidden and against my will".[53] And after his sacrifice and death He has given to Hopkins the acclaim which He withheld during his life.

The Society of Jesus can hardly be reproached for not acclaiming Hopkins as a poet. Indeed Hopkins himself said, "Our Society cannot be blamed for not valuing what it never heard of".[54] The *Month* had, it is true, rejected the only two poems that the priest ever submitted, "The Wreck of the Deutschland" and "The Loss of the Eurydice". But it is very doubtful whether any Victorian magazine would have accepted them. And it should in fairness be remembered that from 1918 (after Bridges had spent twenty-five years in gradually introducing Hopkins into various anthologies and after the critical world had been prepared by the entire movement of modern poetry) it took eight years to dispose of the first edition of some seven hundred copies.

Further, the Jesuits can hardly be blamed for not honouring him as a poet in his lifetime when three of his friends who were poets in their own right withheld any adequate appreciation of him. The story of the relations of Robert Bridges, Canon Dixon, and Coventry Patmore with the poet is an interesting and fascinating one and merits a full study—but it is sufficient here to say that none of them gave him more than a minimum of encouragement.

No one who reads the letters of Canon Dixon can help feeling his beautiful character; but his attitude towards Hopkins' poetry was usually more a matter of astonishment than anything else.

Hopkins' own tender appreciation of Dixon's poetry was due at least in part to a recognition that the Canon's poems had a very slight public: "It is sad to think what disappointment must many times over have filled your heart for the darling children of your mind."[55]

From all the evidence that survives, Bridges too failed to encourage Hopkins, though he had a far greater understanding of his technique than Dixon or even Patmore. Fundamentally there was a great barrier between the two, for Bridges never understood, indeed he very much misunderstood, Hopkins' religious ideals. And these were so much a part of Hopkins that Bridges never touched more than the surface—the metrics and technique —of the man. Abbott has admiringly said that for Bridges "Poetry is in itself a religion". And Oliver Elton has cogently remarked that the central meaning of "The Testament of Beauty" is something like the faith of Prince Myshkin in Dostoevsky's story, that "the world will be saved by beauty". But for Hopkins beauty was not a religion and he didn't feel that he was going to save the world by his poetry. "When we met in London", Hopkins once wrote to Bridges, "we never but once, and then only for a few minutes before parting, spoke on an important subject, but always on literature". But Bridges failed to appreciate even Hopkins the poet.[56]

Coventry Patmore's letters are very disappointing. It was in the summer of 1883 that he met Hopkins at Stonyhurst; after that, with the exception of a week's visit to Patmore at Hastings, during a vacation in England, Hopkins' contact with him was by way of correspondence. Hopkins gave much to him, but Patmore found it impossible to appreciate Hopkins the poet. He did, however, pay tribute to the Jesuit:

> Gerard Hopkins was the only orthodox, and as far as I could see, saintly man in whom religion had absolutely no narrowing effect upon his general opinions and sympathies. A Catholic of the most scrupulous strictness, he could nevertheless see the Holy Spirit in all goodness, truth and beauty; and there was something in all his words and manners which were at once a rebuke and an attraction to all who could only aspire to be like him.[57]

In another place, Patmore admitted, "His character struck me far more than his literary powers".[58]

Certainly then, one cannot censure the editor of the *Month* for failing to recognize Hopkins as a great poet when Robert Bridges, Canon Dixon, and Coventry Patmore failed to do so.

Hopkins gained greatly by his membership of the Society of Jesus. Most important, of course, was the moral and spiritual growth. His membership gave purpose and direction to his entire life and experience. In many ways, it is clear that by constitution and temperament Hopkins was predestined to suffer deeply. The fact that he was a Jesuit did not lessen his anguish; indeed it probably made it keener. But suffering is raised to the dignity of the Cross, to Christ-likeness.

But aside from all moral and spiritual considerations, Hopkins' poetry gained by his joining the Jesuits. It is obvious that quantitatively his output was restricted. But qualitatively it gained in every way. He said he lost the very impulse to write because he had renounced fame, a great spiritual danger. As a result he wrote few poems. But it is to be noted that when he did compose it was because he absolutely had to write and the very qualities which make for the greatness of his poetry and which every critic admires—his absolute honesty, his directness, his passionate personal utterance, his concentrated intensity—are the result of this renunciation. Further, his repudiation of the world allowed him to proceed with amazing independence of conventional standards. Certainly his poetry gained.

T. S. Eliot has suggested that "to be a 'devotional' poet is a limitation", and Hopkins is certainly a religious poet. But it is a limitation to be anything, to have any view of the purpose and meaning of the world. And the mistake is often made of thinking of this as an outside limitation, as something which artificially restricts. Now in the case of Hopkins, the Spiritual Exercises became so much a part of him and of the very pattern of his mind that they no longer restricted; rather they gave significance and direction to all he saw and experienced.

The mistake is often made of considering Jesuit spirituality as a rigid mould. One has only to think of the Jesuit saints to realize how very untrue this is. It should be clear that one of the basic characteristics of the Spiritual Exercises is their great flexibility and adaptability. Since they are, for the most part, concerned with the most fundamental principles of the spiritual life they have a wide inclusiveness. Within them the greatest freedom may be found.

And one has only to compare the qualities of Hopkins' Highgate or Oxford verse with the poetry he wrote as a priest to demonstrate how his spiritual life as a Jesuit gave to his poetry the very qualities which are its greatness.

Modern critics have found this a stumbling-block because they have failed to realize that it is truth that makes man free. John Gould Fletcher doggedly contends: "The question however still arises whether the strict orthodoxy of the Jesuit discipline may not have somewhat limited Hopkins's mind, and whether some other doctrine, capable of a broader and more personal interpretation, could not better serve the turn of those who wish to-day to be marked as his followers." To such a suggestion the words of Arthur Machen might well be countered; in *Hieroglyphics* he wrote:

> You ask me for a new test—or rather for a new expression of the one test—that separates literature from the mass of stuff which is not literature. I will give you a test that will startle you; literature is the expression, through the aesthetic medium of words, of the dogmas of the Catholic Church, and that which in any way is out of harmony with these dogmas is not literature . . . but I tell you that unless you have assimilated the final dogmas— the eternal truths—upon which those things rest, consciously if you please, but subconsciously of necessity, you can never write literature, however clever and amusing you may be. Think of it, and you will see that from the literary standpoint, Catholic dogma is merely the witness, under a special symbolism, of the enduring facts of human nature and the universe; it is merely the voice which tells us distinctly that man is *not* the creature of the drawing-room and the Stock Exchange, but a lonely awful soul confronted by the Source of all Souls, and you will realize that to make literature it is necessary to be, at all events, subconsciously Catholic.

Before we go on to examine the quality and temper of the poems Hopkins wrote while he was in Dublin, we must consider a further factor which had a very pervasive influence during the last years of his life, a condition well known to ascetical writers under the name of "aridity", "spiritual dryness", or "interior desolation". It would be extremely hazardous to estimate the exact cause-and-effect relationship between this condition and his health, his attitude towards his work, and his feeling of impotence, but that it contributed powerfully is certain.

Many who have travelled the road of the spiritual life have found this aridity and desolation to be a very real thing. The layman is prone to attribute all the difficulties of the religious life to natural—however complex—causes. This is tantamount to a denial of the supernatural, and one is reminded of the words Hopkins wrote, words which he might have written to many of his critics: "You do not mean by mystery what a Catholic does. You mean an interesting uncertainty.... But a Catholic by mystery means an incomprehensible certainty."[59] And in lines he wrote during these difficult years the Jesuit warned:

> O the mind, mind has mountains; cliffs of fall
> Frightful, sheer, no-man-fathomed. Hóld them cheap
> May who ne'er hung there.

Hopkins exhibits the suffering and trials which ascetical writers have traditionally attributed to "interior desolation": we shall find his Dublin poems expressing this state, and indications are scattered through his letters and among the notes which he jotted down into an unbound book which is known as the Dublin notebook. One of the most interesting and significant passages occurs in a letter to Bridges in which he attributes his impotence and sterility to the withdrawal of Divine Love from his soul; those who doubt that his poetry is the story of the relationship of his soul to God, that his poems are really love poems, will do well to ponder Hopkins' own words:

> I cannot in conscience spend time on poetry, neither have I the inducements and inspirations that make others compose. Feeling, love in particular, is the great moving power and spring of verse and the only person that I am in love with seldom, especially now, stirs my heart sensibly and when he does I cannot always "make capital" of it, it would be a sacrilege to do so.[60]

And his words, "All impulse fails me.... Nothing comes: I am a eunuch—but it is for the kingdom of heaven's sake", carry the implication that his aridity is a trial sent by heaven.[61]

Some writers have attributed Hopkins' sufferings during his Dublin years to what St. John of the Cross calls the "Dark Night of the Senses" and the "Dark Night of the Soul", which are associated with mysticism.

Now, mystics of all ages have agreed that there is an orderly evolution, a series of stages through which the soul passes as it approaches the mystical experience, the union or "spiritual marriage" with God. There is no mysticism, strictly so-called, before the unitive way. The essence of mysticism, of "infused contemplation" (to speak of it in theologically accurate terms), is, as Père de Grandmaison points out, the felt contact, immediate and experimental without the intrusion of images or the discursive reason, of God's presence: "where this sentiment of immediate presence is wanting there is not, and where it exists there is, mystical contemplation".

The two nights of which St. John of the Cross speaks belong to the unitive way, though the first, the Night of the Senses, is on the borderland between ordinary contemplation and infused contemplation.

The two nights are successive degrees of the contemplation of God, and both involve severe purgations by which the soul is prepared for God. They are called "nights" because God deprives the soul of the use of the ordinary ways of attaining to him which had formerly been satisfactory and at the same time the soul is blinded, as it were, by the new light of infused contemplation. The first, according to St. John of the Cross, prepares the soul for the lower reaches of the unitive life (quietude) and the second, the Dark Night of the Soul, designates the sum-total of all the trials and sufferings which precede the spiritual marriage.

Both nights involve great aridity, desolation, and trials, for their purpose is to detach the soul from all (the life of the senses, the discursive reason, the will; all self-love; all love of the consolations of God instead of the God of Consolations) that stands between it and its union with God in the unitive way. Sometimes the two nights are summarized by saying that the first subjects the senses to the intellect, and the second subjects the intellect to God. Sometimes it is said that the two nights are simply two kinds of sufferings: the purpose of the first made up of aridity, darkness, etc.; the second of a far more painful ordeal.

But Père Poulain has shown that all such attempts to characterize the two nights of St. John of the Cross in terms of the trials they involve miss the very distinguishing characteristic:

> These states are the cause of sufferings; but the sufferings are a secondary element only, a consequence. People make mistakes about this sometimes because of the difficulty of defining the exact nature of the principal element, the contemplation of God. They prefer only to consider the sufferings which have nothing mysterious about them (aridity, the sight of our sins, etc.). In a word, instead of endeavouring to penetrate into the saint's real meaning,

they are satisfied with adapting his language to ordinary things
which are already familiar to them.

But the chief element of both the Dark Night of the Senses and
the Dark Night of the Soul is that in them God is beginning to
communicate (however intermittently or confusedly) the essence
of the unitive way: the immediate awareness of God's presence in
the soul.

Not a single line of Hopkins that is extant bears the authentic
stamp of the very essence of the Dark Night of the Senses or of
the Soul. He is not in any strict sense a contemplative or mystical
poet. The sufferings and trials and aridities and desolations which
he endured and which we shall see so poignantly expressed in his
Dublin poems are not *the* characteristics of the mystical life and
are shared by earlier stages of the spiritual road to perfection.

I have said that Hopkins was not a mystical writer or a mystical
poet. This is not to deny that he may have been a mystic, for he
may never have expressed that which constitutes the essence of
the mystic: the immediate awareness of God's presence in the soul.
He may have considered it "a sacrilege" to speak of such things,
as indeed he intimates in his letter to Bridges on love as "the
great moving power and spring of verse". He had a deep reticence
about some things. When he came to commenting on some of
Coventry Patmore's Psyche Odes, he confessed, "I feel it as
dangerous to criticize them almost as the Canticles".[62] When
Patmore showed the Jesuit his prose tract *Sponsa Dei* which,
apparently, treated of "the relation of the soul to Christ as his
betrothed wife", Hopkins said, "That's telling secrets".[63]
(Hopkins, I think, has been freed of any real responsibility
for Patmore's subsequent destruction of the manuscript.) It
may be, then, that Hopkins chose never to indicate his own
experience of the mystical state. But until evidence is produced to show that he himself experienced the unitive way it is
certainly inaccurate to attribute the aridity and desolation which
is the subject of many of his poems to the Dark Night of the Soul.
Only by using the word in a very loose and inaccurate sense may
Hopkins be called a mystic. This is not to deny, of course, that
he was a saintly man.

While it would be inaccurate to say that Hopkins' life, his
letters and note-books, and his poems show that he experienced
the Dark Night of the Soul, it is clear that he did go through a

period of very torturing "spiritual desolation"—and many of the trials and sufferings connected with it are analogous to and are shared by those who have suffered in the two nights.

But the aridity or desolation which Hopkins suffered has a far wider application. "This is nothing new nor strange unto them that have experience in the way of God", says the author of the *Imitation of Christ*. And Sister Madeleva, who has made a survey of "spiritual dryness" in ascetical writers contemporary with the Pearl-poet, refers to it as "perhaps one of the commonest of all trials in the spiritual life and one on which almost every spiritual writer has had something to say". She has collected instances from scores of spiritual writers.

But here it seems useless to accumulate quotations and excerpts to prove the existence and characteristics of such a state. It is not a matter, in the case of Hopkins, of influences or of direct parallels. But since we shall find that his Dublin poems are a magnificent expression of his spiritual desolation, it is necessary to point out briefly its general aspects.

We shall study this condition through three authors: St. Ignatius, Hopkins' own particular master; the author of the *Imitation*, whom above all other spiritual writers St. Ignatius commended to his followers; and lastly, the writings of Marie Lataste (1822-47), a French nun of the Congregation of the Sacred Heart, who had received from the lips of Christ instructions forming a complete spiritual and doctrinal education; she had been buried at Roehampton and her works published by the Fathers of the Society of Jesus. Hopkins frequently read her in his last years, and his Commentary on the Exercises is filled with references to her.

St. Ignatius appended to the Spiritual Exercises a short study of aridity. He sketches the characteristics of "spiritual desolation" by contrasting it with "spiritual consolation". He begins by telling what is meant by the latter:

> I call it consolation when some interior movement in the soul is caused, through which the soul comes to be inflamed with love of its Creator and Lord; and when it can in consequence love no created thing on the face of the earth in itself, but in the Creator of them all. . . . I call consolation every increase of hope, faith and charity, and all interior joy which calls and attracts to heavenly things and to the salvation of one's soul, quieting it and giving it peace in its Creator and Lord.

In commenting on this passage, the Directory remarks further that it is

> of such a nature that while it is present, acts of virtue are exercised easily, and even with sweetness, delight, and warm affections. ... It has various manifestations and component elements, as for instance peace and a certain interior ·quiet, spiritual joy, light, a clearer knowledge of divine things, tears, elevation of the mind to God, steadfast hope in God, perception of eternal realities, heavenly-mindedness, warmth of holy love.

In contrast, says St. Ignatius in the Exercises, is spiritual desolation:

> I call desolation all the contrary ... such as darkness of soul, disturbance in it, movement to things low and earthly, the disquiet of different agitations and temptations, moving to want of confidence, without hope, without love, when one finds oneself all lazy, tepid, sad, and as if separated from his Creator and Lord.

Of this state the *Imitation* says:

> It is no hard matter to despise human comfort, when we have that which is divine.
> It is much and very much, to be able to lack both human and divine comfort; and, for God's honour, to be willing cheerfully to endure desolation of heart; and to seek oneself in nothing, nor to regard one's own merit.

Christ says the very same thing to Marie Lataste:

> It is easy, my daughter, for the soul to be joyous and fervent when it experiences the consolations flowing from the grace of God. But for a soul to be joyous and fervent when God seems to have withdrawn from it, when it feels its weakness and wretchedness, when it is troubled and depressed, when its mind is harassed with a thousand perplexing thoughts, when it finds itself distracted in prayer, and feels itself heavy and drowsy in the service of God— this, My daughter, is a thing rare to meet with, and yet it ought not to be so ... know how to submit entirely and in all things to the will and good pleasure of God.

Such quotations could be multiplied endlessly; the following is one from St. John of the Cross which characterizes desolation in general:

> The soul is conscious of a profound emptiness and destitution of the three kinds of goods, natural, temporal, and spiritual, which

are ordained for its comfort; it sees itself in the midst of the opposite evils, miserable imperfections and aridities, emptiness of the understanding and abandonment of the spirit in darkness.

Spiritual writers are agreed that when God visits the soul with aridity, it is in order to detach the soul from all created things and even from the happiness derived from devotion, so that the soul may learn to love God for His sake alone; "God, in acting thus", says Marie Lataste, "desires to detach him in order to unite him to Himself and to be his sovereign good". He wants to humble us. He wants to effect a purification from past faults, present attachments, and all manner of self-seeking. One lives in a sort of torpor and acts only by sheer force of will. When one has to serve God without any relish, on principle and by sheer will-power, one suffers keenly, and the suffering becomes an act of expiation and atonement.

One of the purposes of spiritual desolation, say the Spiritual Exercises, is "to try us and see how much we are and how much we let ourselves out in His service and praise without such great pay of consolation and great graces". Another, continues the founder of the Jesuits, is

> to give us true acquaintance and knowledge, that we may interiorly feel that it is not ours to get or keep great devotion, intense love, tears, or any other spiritual consolation, but that all is the gift and grace of God our Lord, and that we may not build a nest in a thing not ours, raising our intellect into some pride or vainglory, attributing to ourselves devotion or the other things of spiritual consolation.

And, once more, Marie Lataste merely supplements this when she says that God "seems sometimes to retire with His graces, His consolations, His strength, and His support; He leaves souls to themselves, that they may be sensible of their misery and nothingness, in order also to make them continue striving, to exercise them for battle, to prove to them how powerless they are without Him, and to increase their merits".

One of the most valuable effects of "spiritual desolation", writers on the religious life agree, is the humility it produces. The individual feels that God has abandoned him and casts about for reasons for His apparent desertion and usually locates it in his own unworthiness. The soul begins to understand its own feebleness. Spiritual dangers abound, for the soul, believing itself abandoned, is tempted to weariness and despair; we shall see how the *Imitation* and the Exercises try to guard against these. But the detachment from all self-seeking and the acknowledgement of unworthiness are positive spiritual fruits of this trial. "He that is taught by the gift of grace, and schooled by the withdrawing thereof", says the *Imitation*, "will not dare to attribute any good to himself, but will rather acknowledge himself to be poor and naked".

The antidotes most frequently suggested for "spiritual desolation" are trust in God and His grace, patience, humble resignation and abandonment to the will of God.

"Let him who is in desolation", St. Ignatius advised, "labour to be in patience, which is contrary to the vexations which come to him." The *Imitation* admonishes: "At such a time there is no better remedy than patience, and the denying of myself according to the will of God."

Despair must be combated vigorously, and the soul must resign itself to the will of God, suffering in union with Christ. Such is the difficult teaching of that great handbook of the spiritual life, the *Imitation of Christ*:

> For when the grace of God cometh unto a man, then he is able for all things. And when it goeth away, then is he poor and weak, and as it were left only for affliction.
> In this case thou oughtest not to be cast down, nor to despair; but to resign thyself calmly to the will of God, and whatever comes upon thee, to endure it for the glory of Jesus Christ.

St. Ignatius in the Spiritual Exercises suggests that we fight desolation "by insisting more on prayer, meditation, on much examination, and by giving ourselves more scope in some suitable way of doing penance".

The spiritually depressed soul is urged to imitate Christ, who "being in agony, prayed the longer". In the midst of all his despondency and impotence, his fatigue and stagnation, his purification and trial, the well-advised soul, says the *Imitation*, "doth not by any means despair, but more earnestly beseecheth the Lord, and saith, 'Unto Thee, O Lord, will I cry, and I will pray unto my God'."

Such are the general backgrounds, the characteristics, and the antidotes for the crucifying spiritual aridity and desolation with which Hopkins was tortured during at least part of his residence in Dublin, when his life became a purgatory—when the only person he was in love with had withdrawn His love and consolations. The whole world around him became insipid, he considered himself a failure, he lost his inclinations towards and pleasures in ordinary occupations, he was filled with tedium and sadness.

But there is a more positive aspect to this whole period of Hopkins' severe suffering and trial—and this must be constantly emphasized. "Suffering", said Eternal Wisdom to Blessed Henry Suso, "is the ancient law of love. There is no quest without pain, there is no lover who is not also a martyr." The problem of suffering is indeed one which well-nigh baffles the human intellect. One has only to think of Calvary to realize how inadequate are most explanations. St. Ignatius, like other masters of the spiritual life, found the meaning of suffering in its spiritual value. "If God gives you an abundant harvest of trial", he said, "it is a sign of the great holiness which He desires you to attain". Paradoxically, Hopkins had written to Bridges consoling him for his sister's painful death: "But sufferings falling on such a person as your sister was are to be looked on as the marks of God's particular love and this is truer the more exceptional they are." And in 1884-5 he was jotting down in his "Dublin Note-Book" (an unprinted miscellany of notes, into which a few spiritual annotations found their way) the following proposition to meditate: "The love of the Son for the Father leads him to take a created nature and in that to offer him sacrifice."[65]

In "The Wreck of the Deutschland", his first Jesuit poem, he had realized that trial and suffering bring the soul "to hero of Calvary, Christ's feet", and for his twenty-one years in the Society the Spiritual Exercises had held before him the ideal of sacrifice and suffering in union with Christ as the highest perfection on earth. Such, too, is the burden of an untitled fragment in which he wrote:

> Hope holds to Christ the mind's own mirroi out
> To take His lovely likeness more and more.
> It will not well, so she would bring about
> An ever brighter burnish than before
> And turns to wash it from her welling eyes
> And breathes the blots off all with sighs on sighs.

During these troubled years only the example of Christ offered him any consolation. In 1886 he wrote in a tender letter to Canon Dixon:

See how ... Christ our Lord ... was cut short ... his plans were baffled, his hopes dashed, and his work was done by being broken off undone. However much he understood all this he found it an intolerable grief to submit to it. He left the example.[66]

It was to Christ that Hopkins looked in his own agony; he endeavoured to take up his cross to follow Him even beyond the garden.

Hopkins had heard Christ say that if he would enter into His Kingdom, he must first drink of His chalice. Truly the *Imitation* says:

> Jesus hath now many lovers of His heavenly kingdom, but few bearers of His Cross.
>
> He hath many desirous of consolation, but few of tribulation.
>
> He findeth many companions of His table, but few of His abstinence.
>
> All desire to rejoice with Him, few are willing to endure any thing for Him.
>
> Many follow Jesus unto the breaking of bread; but few to the drinking of the cup of His passion.

Hopkins was one who endeavoured to follow: he did not always succeed, but he was capable of bowing his head and saying, as he does in his "Dublin Note-Book" from the depths of his suffering: "And the other things on earth—take it that weakness, ill health, every cross is a help." Then, after this passage, he invokes the words of Christ in his agony, "The Chalice which my Father hath given me, shall I not drink it?" A few lines later Hopkins returns the answer: "Consider ... how the joy of seeing Christ our Lord is from having lived for him."[67]

On a religious plane Hopkins' life becomes heroic rather than tragic, for his is the life of Christ. However much we may be inclined to regret his thinning stream of poetry, we must transcend the values of mere art and "bring in the infinite":

> Surf, snow, river and earth
> Gnashed: but thou art above, thou Orion of light;
> Thy unchancelling poising palms were weighing the worth,
> Thou martyr-master: in thy sight
> Storm flakes were scroll-leaved flowers, lily showers—sweet heaven
> was astrew in them.

Last Poems (*1884–9*)

"WE cannot apprehend a work of literature", says Mr. Middleton Murry, "except as a manifestation of the rhythm of the soul of the man who created it. If we stop short of that, our understanding is incomplete." Hopkins' last poems are deeply expressive of his religious life during those last five years.

Three poems of 1884-6 serve as an introduction to the most personal and possibly the greatest of all his poems, his seven sonnets of 1884-5, which form a well-integrated group. The three poems, in powerfully re-emphasizing a previous theme, connect his earlier productions with those of his Dublin period. "To what serves Mortal Beauty?", "On the Portrait of Two Beautiful Young People", and "Spelt from Sibyl's Leaves" all stress the overwhelming importance of the spiritual; this motif has frequently recurred in his poems, but now it is expressed with a new and impassioned clarity and vigour.

All other considerations become dwarfed in comparison with his emphasis on the "handsome heart". Yet it must not be thought that he was rejecting natural beauty. He still considered it good, but a good subordinate to the beauty of the soul. This is affirmed in both "To what serves Mortal Beauty?" and "On the Portrait of Two Beautiful Young People". The first was written in 1885, probably the same year as "Spelt from Sibyl's Leaves" and during the same month (August, 1885) as many of the autobiographical sonnets which we shall study after we have looked at these poems. "On the Portrait of Two Beautiful Young People" was written a year later.

In the first of these poems, Hopkins recognizes both the danger and justification of natural beauty. The poem is cryptic and chopped, conveying quick, jerky, shot-like impacts of impressions and ideas. It opens with the question which its title suggests:

> To what serves mortal beauty¹ —dangerous; does set danc-
> ing blood—the O-seal-that-so¹ feature,* flung prouder form
> Than Purcell tune lets tread to?

* Suggests the classical beauty of the head on a coin.

In "The Leaden Echo and the Golden Echo" he had implied that natural beauty has about it something "dearly and dangerously sweet"; the Jesuit realized that for the artistic temperament, keenly sensitive to the attractiveness of the created world, beauty tends to become an exclusive end, to entangle the will and divert the soul from enjoying God in all things and all things in God. That is the danger any artist has to face, and if he is a priest at the same time, then the tension at times may prove doubly difficult. Yet, as we have so frequently seen, Hopkins does not reject or despise created beauty; he realizes fully the haunting beauty of God's handiwork.

Having posited the initial question, the poem proceeds to answer by saying that mortal beauty can tell man "what good means":

> See: it does this: keeps warm
> Men's wits to the things that are; ǀ what good means—where* a glance
> Master more may than gaze, ǀ gaze out of countenance.
> Those lovely lads once, wet fresh ǀ windfalls of war's storm,
> How then should Gregory, a father, ǀ have gleanéd else from swarm-
> ed Rome? But God to a nation ǀ dealt that day's dear chance.

In the lines immediately succeeding he is anxious to set up, once more, his hierarchy of inscapes:

> To man, that needs would worship ǀ block or barren stone,
> Our law says: Love what are ǀ love's worthiest, were all known;
> World's loveliest—men's selves. Self ǀ flashes off frame and face.

Then comes the full answer to the question, "To what serves mortal beauty?"—an answer which warns us not to become inordinately attached to beauty; a warning, however, to recognize beauty for what it is, yet not to stop with mere admiration but to go a step further and pray that mortal beauty be crowned by transcendent beauty:

> What do then? how meet beauty? ǀ Merely meet it; own,
> Home at heart, heaven's sweet gift; ǀ then leave, let that alone.
> Yes, wish that though, wish all, ǀ God's better beauty, grace.

This involves the hard task—as I have said, particularly difficult for the artist—of giving due admiration to the beauty of this world but yet affirming its subordination to eternal beauty. Baron von

---

* i.e. (tells) what good means—(especially in such cases) where etc.

Hügel has expressed the paradoxical exaction of this attitude with great precision:

> The very things we, men, are to love and seek are also the same things which we are to be detached from, and from which we are to flee. Attachment and cultivation, detachment and renouncement, will thus each gain and keep a splendid spaciousness of occasions and materials. There will be no fanaticism, but a profound earnestness; there will be no worldliness, but an immense variety of interest and expansion towards all things in their specific kinds and degrees of goodness, truth, and beauty.

Such was the delicate balance which Hopkins strove to maintain; very probably he did not always succeed, but the effort to find the correct solution lies behind many of his letters and many of his poems. And now, in "To what serves Mortal Beauty?" he stops to admire beauty as "heaven's sweet gift", but then goes on to utter the prayer that the self that wears it may attain "God's better beauty, grace". For we know that, according to Hopkins, the self reaches the highest perfection when it co-operates with grace and becomes another Christ,

> Acts in God's eye what in God's eye he is—
> Christ—for Christ plays in ten thousand places,
> Lovely in limbs, and lovely in eyes not his
> To the Father through the features of men's faces.

The stress on the overwhelming importance of the spiritual in comparison with just natural beauty is the main theme of an unfinished poem, "On the Portrait of Two Beautiful Young People".

In a letter to Canon Dixon he tells of the origin of the poem:

> I was at Xmas and New Year down with some kind people in Co. Kildare, where I happened to see the portrait of two beautiful young persons, a brother and sister, living in the neighbourhood. It so much struck me that I began an elegy.

The opening stanzas are an appreciation of the art which has captured and crystallized for ever the beauty and innocence of the young pair, "a joy for ever". But a joy suffused with a gentle melancholy at the realization that beauty passes: "And beauty's dearest veriest vein is tears".

But how much more terrifying is the priest's realization that innocence, too, passes and becomes corrupt! The beauty of the

youthful pair sinks into insignificance when he turns to consider
the far more important matter of their spiritual beauty. He gently
yet firmly addresses them:

> Where lies your landmark, seamark, or soul's star?
> There's none but truth can stead you. Christ is truth.

And evil is especially apt to attack the beauty of innocence:

> Your feast of; that most in you earnest eye
> May but call on your banes to more carouse.
> Worst will the best.* What worm was here, we cry,
> To have havoc-pocked so, see, the hung-heavenward boughs?

"Spelt from Sibyl's Leaves" is far more personal and serves as a
direct introduction to the sonnets of 1884–5. It expresses the
terrible lucidity with which the Jesuit priest was seeing the
necessity of rooting out every inordinate affection on his road to
spiritual perfection. In the edition of Hopkins' poems, Bridges
conjectured that the piece was written in 1881; but this is very
improbable, for what seems to be a first draft appears in the
"Dublin Note-Book" of 1884–5 and the experience reflected in
the poem brings it into proximity to the struggle Hopkins was
fighting during his years in Dublin. It is typical of the intense
introspection of a soul in desolation, when it casts about to find a
reason for its desertion and fastens upon its own unworthiness.

When he was writing his Commentary on the Exercises Hopkins
had remarked: "There is a way of thinking of past sin such that
the thought numbs and kills the heart", and now in Dublin in the
midst of the lassitude and stagnation which accompany aridity
he made an intense effort to apply the "Examen" of the Spiritual
Exercises to himself; in his "Dublin Note-book" he put down:
"I must ask God to strengthen my faith or I shall never keep the
particular examen. I must say the stations for this intention.
Resolve also to keep it particularly even in the present state of
lethargy."[2]

In "Spelt from Sibyl's Leaves" the fading of the dappled day-
time world into night becomes the symbol of the time when
there are two all-important and inescapable categories: "black,
white; right, wrong." In the poem Hopkins' art reaches new

---

* That which is most attractive in you, your beauty and goodness, may be
only a danger which will intensify your tendency toward evil "(your banes").
The worst will corrupt the very best (powers or persons).

heights. "The poem opens", Mr. F. R. Leavis has sensitively written,

> with evening deepening into night. We are not merely told that evening "strains", we feel evening straining, to become night, enveloping everything, in the movement, the progression of alliteration, assonance, and rime. This progression is associated with, and hardly distinguishable from, the development of meaning in the sequence of adjectives: evening is first sweetly solemn, serene, etherealizing and harmonizing, then becomes less tranquillizing and more awful, and finally ends in the blackness of night.

Prepared to observe the subtle nuances of the verse, we may look at the poem which opens, as Morton Zabel has remarked, with a single progression which encompasses man's life-cycle with order and fluidity:

> Earnest, earthless, equal, attuneable, ǀ vaulty, voluminous, . . . stupendous
> Evening strains to be time's vást, ǀ womb-of-all home-of-all, hearse-of-all night.

It proceeds to lines of cumulative beauty:

> Her fond yellow hornlight wound to the west, ǀ her wild hollow hoarlight hung to the height
> Waste; her earliest stars, earl-stars, ǀ stárs principal, overbend us,
> Fire-féaturing heaven. For earth ǀ her being has unbound, her dapple is at an end, as-
> tray or aswarm, all throughther, in throngs; ǀ self in self steepéd and páshed—quite
> Disremémbering, dísmémbering ǀ áll now.

Then the poet, with dreadful clarity, sees this as a symbol of the time when only two categories shall encompass all other considerations, Two Standards:

> Heart, you round me right
> With: Our évening is over us; óur night ǀ whélms, whélms, ánd will end us.
> Only the beak-leaved boughs dragonish ǀ damask the tool-smooth bleak light; black,
> Ever so black on it. Óur tale, O óur oracle! ǀ Lét life, wáned, ah lét life wind

Off hér once skéined stained véined variety ˡ upon, áll on twó spools;
   párt, pen, páck
Now her áll in twó flocks, twó folds—black, white; ˡ right, wrong,
   reckon but, reck but, mind
But thése two; wáre* of a wórld where but these ˡ twó tell, each off
   the óther; of a rack
Where, selfwrung, selfstrung, sheathe-and shelterless,† ˡ thóughts
   agáinst thoughts in groans grind.‡

The bitter self-knowledge of the last lines echoes Hopkins' own
probing of his soul during a period in which he found it desolate
and unworthy. His keen self-criticism was part of his torture and
crucifixion.

"Spelt from Sibyl's Leaves" prepares us for a group of seven
sonnets written in 1884-5; they are without titles and not dated,
though probably they were written for the most part during the
summer of 1885.

These seven sonnets are among the most personal and intro-
spective of all Hopkins' verse. They bear the marks of having
issued from his soul in a catharsis of his burdened spirit. He tells
their story in a letter to Bridges: "I shall shortly have some sonnets
to send you, five or more. Four of these came like inspirations
unbidden and against my will. And in the life I lead now, which
is one of a continually jaded and harassed mind, if in any leisure
I try to do anything I make no way—nor with my work, alas!
but so it must be."[3] All of them impress the reader as expressions
of a man anxious to unload his desolate heart.

Indeed they were born of the trial and suffering of the complicated "winter world" in which he lived in Dublin. The poems
are a corroboration of the "spiritual desolation" which was outlined in the previous chapter. They were wrung from him amid

* Aware, but also suggesting beware.
† Sheatheless and shelterless.
‡ F. R. Leavis has a fine appreciation of these lines: "The 'yellow hornlight'
is, of course, the setting moon; 'fond'—tender, soft, sympathetic, clinging as if
reluctant to go. . . . The 'hoarlight' is the cold, hard starlight, 'wild' and 'hollow'—remote, inhuman, a kind of emptiness in the hollow vault—in contrast
to the 'fond yellow' moonlight. . . . The 'dapple' of earth . . . has gone, merged
('throughther'—each through other) into neutrality. . . . He suddenly realizes
the whole thing as a parable. . . . His heart 'rounds' him, i.e. whispers (as in
the ballads), and 'rounds upon him' with the thought that . . . the trees are
no longer the beautiful, refreshing things of daylight, they have turned fan-
tastically strange, hard and cruel, 'beak-leaved' suggesting the cold, hard light,
steel-like gleam of polished tools, against which they appear as a kind of
damascene-work ('damask') on a blade." *New Bearings in English Poetry*, pp.
183-5.

the prostrating anguish of ill-health, uncongenial surroundings, the tedium of heavy routine-duties, the depression of mental fatigue, and the sterility and impotence which constituted his spiritual aridity when he felt that his God had withdrawn His Love. Then the soul, spiritual writers tell us and Hopkins' poems rehearse, feels deserted and abandoned; then it is that the soul fixes upon the bitter knowledge of its own feebleness and unworthiness. Amid such sufferings we find Hopkins' intense moral struggle to live the Exercises and the Rules of the Society at a time when everything is difficult. He endeavours to root out all "self-love, will and interest" and patiently abandon himself to the Will of God. He experiences the agony of drinking his bitter chalice with Christ.

Hopkins referred to one of these poems as "written in blood", but he might have applied the phrase to all seven of these sonnets. All are highly autobiographical, throbbing with passionate utterance. To them the reader could aptly attach the lines which Hopkins wrote of Purcell:

> It is the forged feature finds me; it is the rehearsal
> Of own, of abrupt self there so thrusts on, so throngs the ear.

In each of these poems Hopkins reforges his own experience with his own soul, giving his expression an inscape of its own, bleak, majestic, terrible. The lines he now writes are astringent in their chastened severity. Concentrated and compressed, the verse is simple yet direct. Nothing is hesitating, nothing is tentative. Even the most severe critics of the Jesuit have had to grant that here is his greatest poetry. The distinctive religious meaning and the distinctive aesthetic value interpenetrate and fuse.

The first of these sonnets (No. 44) gives a partial inventory of his trials during this period when Christ was playing the double role of afflictor and helper. Straightforward and matter-of-fact are the opening lines:

> To seem the stranger lies my lot, my life
> Among strangers. Father and mother dear,
> Brothers and sisters are in Christ not near
> And he my peace my parting, sword and strife.

But though he regrets leaving his friends behind him in a land he loves, his Irish exile is not his severest suffering:

England, whose honour O all my heart woos, wife
To my creating thought, would neither hear
Me, were I pleading, plead nor do I: I wear-
y of idle a being but by* where wars are rife.
    I am in Ireland now; now I am at a third
Remove. Not but in all removes I can
Kind love both give and get.

The verse tightens as he plumbs a deeper affliction:

Only what word
Wisest my heart breeds dark heaven's baffling ban
Bars or hell's spell thwarts. This to hoard unheard,
Heard unheeded, leaves me a lonely began.†

Yet the painful bafflement of these lines comes nearer to un-
ravelling in the explicitness of his next sonnet; for in that he
develops the implications of his reference to Christ as "my peace
my parting, sword and strife". It is the cry of that anguished
aridity and "spiritual desolation" which has been characterized
in the last chapter. Indeed, St. Ignatius' description of this state
of the soul is the prose counterpart of the octet of the sonnet. In
the Exercises he had written: "I call desolation . . . darkness of
the soul, disturbance in it . . . the disquiet of different agitations . . .
moving to want of confidence, without hope, without love, when
one finds oneself all lazy, tepid, sad, and as if separated from his
Creator and Lord." "With witness", cries Hopkins in the poem
(No. 45), "I speak this":

I wake and feel the fell of dark,‡ not day.
What hours, O what black hours we have spent
This night! what sights you, heart, saw; ways you went!
And more must, in yet longer light's delay.
    With witness I speak this. But where I say
Hours I mean years, mean life. And my lament
Is cries countless, cries like dead letters sent
To dearest him that lives alas! away.

One of the greatest tortures of the soul suffering "spiritual desolation", St. John of the Cross tells us, "is the thought that God
has abandoned it, of which it had no doubt; that He cast it away
into darkness as an abominable thing . . . the shadow of death and

---

* i.e. I who am weary of being such a one as only stands idly by.
† As Bridges has suggested: leaves me a lonely [one who only] began.
‡ Suggests both the covering of night and the preterite of *fall*.

the pains and torments of hell are most acutely felt, that is, the
sense of being without God. . . . All this and even more the soul
feels now, for a fearful apprehension has come upon it that thus
it will be with it for ever".

This is a superb commentary on the sestet; now, self "tastes
self"·

> I am gall, I am heartburn. God's most deep decree
> Bitter would have me taste: my taste was me;
> Bones built in me, flesh filled, blood brimmed the curse.
> Selfyeast of spirit a dull dough sours. I see
> The lost are like this, and their scourge to be
> As I am mine, their sweating selves; but worse.*

The terrible agony of his desolation, from which there seems
to be no relief, makes him cry out in another poem (No. 41) that
there can be no trial worse than abandonment:

> No worst, there is none. Pitched past pitch of grief,
> More pangs will, schooled at forepangs, wilder wring.

And he appeals to the silent heavens:

> Comforter, where, where is your comforting?
> Mary, mother of us, where is your relief?

But again he turns with terrifying directness to the only answer he
seemed to get:

> My cries heave, herds-long; huddle in a main, a chief
> Woe, world-sorrow; on an age-old anvil wince and sing—
> Then lull, then leave off. Fury had shrieked "No ling-
> ering! Let me be fell: force I must be brief."

Then the lines warn us not to underestimate the sufferings endured during the absence of the Comforter. The poem closes
with small comfort:

> O the mind, mind has mountains; cliffs of fall
> Frightful, sheer, no-man-fathomed. Hold them cheap
> May who† ne'er hung there. Nor does long our small
> Durance deal with that steep or deep. Here! creep,
> Wretch, under a comfort serves‡ in a whirlwind: all
> Life death does end and each day dies with sleep.

* "But (their condition is even) worse" or "but worse (is yet to come)"
† He may hold them cheap who, etc.
‡ i.e. under a comfort that serves.

In such thoughts he comes near to the precipice of despair. No wonder that spiritual writers who have dealt with "interior desolation" have warned against utter hopelessness. St. Ignatius had tried to protect the desolate heart from despairing, and the author of the *Imitation* had urged: "Thou oughtest not to be cast down, nor to despair; but resign thyself calmly to the will of God, and whatever comes upon thee, to endure it for the glory of Jesus Christ." Such is Hopkins' resolve in a sonnet to which Bridges gave the title "Carrion Comfort". In the opening lines the poet rejects Despair with the little strength left in him:

> Not, I'll not, carrion comfort, Despair, not feast on thee;
> Not untwist—slack they may be—these last strands of man
> In me ór, most weary, cry *I can no more.*

And he summons every effort of his will to cry out:

> I can;
> Can something, hope, wish day come, not choose not to be.

He asks, in imagery powerful in its recreation of the violence of the demon he has been wrestling with, the reason for his trial:

> But ah, but O thou terrible, why wouldst thou rude on me
> Thy wring-world right foot rock? lay a lionlimb against me? scan
> With darksome devouring eyes my bruiséd bones? and fan,
> O in turns of tempest, me heaped there; me frantic to avoid thee and.
> flee?

And he gives the answer, succint in its austerity, in the line immediately following: he recognizes that his suffering comes from God that he may be purged. He affirms the spiritual justification of his crucifixion:

> Why? That my chaff might fly; my grain lie, sheer and clear.

Then comes the paradoxical satisfaction of having kissed the hand that whipped him, the joy that comes from abandonment of all self-will, from the submission and acceptance and identification with the divine will—like the nun in "The Wreck of the Deutschland": "the Cross she calls Christ to her, christens her wild-worst Best". The desolate soul in the *Imitation* prays, "Behold, O beloved Father, I am in Thy hands, under the rod of Thy correction I bow myself". And Christ says to Marie Lataste: "God in heaven is for man a physician who slays to make alive, who strikes to heal." There is joy in the closing lines of "Carrion Comfort":

Nay in all that toil, that coil, since (seems) I kissed the rod,
Hand rather,* my heart lo! lapped strength, stole joy, would laugh,
    chéer.
Cheer whom though? the hero whose heaven-handling flung me,
    fóot tród
Me? or me that fought him? O which one? is it each one? That
    night, that year
Of now done darkness I wretch lay wrestling with (my God!) my
    God.

He recognizes that "spiritual consolation" can come only from
God and that he himself is helpless and impotent. In one of these
sonnets (No. 47) his tormented soul confesses its own inability
to find comfort:

> I cast for comfort I can no more get
> By groping round my comfortless, than blind
> Eyes in their dark can day.†

He calls a halt to his distress as he realizes that comfort can come
only from the Source of all Solace. St. Ignatius had said that one
of the purposes of "spiritual desolation" is "that we may inter-
iorly feel that it is not ours to get or keep ... spiritual consolation, but that all is the gift and grace of God our Lord". The
Imitation had advised: "As for comforts, leave them to God; let
Him do therein as shall best please Him." Such (No. 47) is
Hopkins' own humble resignation and trust in God's grace:

> Soul, self; come, poor Jackself,‡ I do advise
> You, jaded, let be; call off thoughts awhile
> Elsewhere; leave comfort root-room; let joy size
> At God knows when to God knows what; whose smile
> 's not wrung, see you; unforeseen times rather§—as skies
> Betweenpie mountains—lights a lovely mile.

Indeed he comes to see that the soul must attain the virtues
of patience among its trials and desolations.

---

* Since, so it seems to me at least, I kissed the rod, or rather I should say,
the hand that punished me, etc.
† As Bridges has suggested: I search for comfort which I can no more find
by groping around my comfortless world than a blind man can find day in his
dark world.
‡ Mildly deprecatory.
§ As Laura Riding and Robert Graves suggest: "Joy comes suddenly and
unexpectedly as when, walking among mountains, you come to a point where
the sky shines through a cleft between two mountains and throws a shaft of
light over a mile of ground thus unexpectedly illuminated for you."

The Exercises insisted: "Let him who is in desolation labour to be in patience", and the *Imitation* admonished, "Dispose thyself to patience rather than to comfort... All men recommend patience; few, however, they are who are willing to suffer", and again, "We are always willing to have something for our comfort; and with difficulty a man doth strip himself of self". Now Hopkins himself goes through the agonizing submission:

> Patience, hard thing! the hard thing but to pray,
> But bid for, Patience is!

He specifies the demands of the bitter cup:

> Patience who asks
> Wants war, wants wounds; weary his times, his tasks;
> To do without, take tosses, and obey.*

No words could more tersely convey the sense of his own difficulties during this period. They are stark and direct in their truth. Still, his reason proceeds to tell him:

> Rare patience roots in these, and, these away,
> Nowhere. Natural heart's ivy, Patience masks
> Our ruins of wrecked past purpose. There she basks†
> Purple eyes and seas of liquid leaves all day.

He realizes that to pray for Patience is to ask for the rack:

> We hear our hearts grate on themselves: it kills
> To bruise them dearer

Still the priest asks God for the death of self-will. His difficult prayer is that of Christ: "Not what I will, but what thou wilt." With St. Ignatius he repeats: "Take, Lord, and receive all my liberty, my memory, my intellect and all my will.... All is thine, dispose of it according to Thy will"; and he completes the submission to the divine will:

> We hear our hearts grate on themselves: it kills
> To bruise them dearer. Yet the rebellious wills
> Of us we do bid God bend to him even so.

---

* Patience who demands of one that he suffer war and wounds; who asks these things of one who is weary of his activities, his tasks, his deprivations, his disappointments, his obediences.

† The image is of Patience who covers over the ruined structures of our former hopes and plans; she is "natural heart's ivy" and this ivy with its "purple eyes and seas of liquid leaves", "basks" contentedly on our ruined purposes "all day".

And God is not far off with the deliverance:

> And where is he who more and more distils
> Delicious kindness?—He is patient. Patience fills
> His crisp combs,* and that comes those ways we know.

The poem thus ends with a calm which has followed upon the priest's complete resignation. And we must realize, though Hopkins was too humble to say so himself, that the final lines of another sonnet (No. 39) of 1885, which he applied to all who struggle to attain perfection, apply to him as well. Christ from above looks down upon the warfare in the world:

> There he bides in bliss
> Now, and seeing somewhére some mán do all that man can do,
> For love he leans forth, needs his neck must fall on, kiss,
> And cry "O Christ-done deed!, So God-made-flesh does too:
> Were I come o'er again" cries Christ "it should be this."

Such are these seven sonnets of desolation. However complex and interrelated were the factors in his life which form the background for these poems, Hopkins interpreted his suffering in terms of "spiritual desolation" and endeavoured to deal with his trials as spiritual writers of all ages had advised. This is not, of course, to deny that natural causes may have contributed to his torture; but God's providence may operate through perfectly ordinary means; and further, as Père Poulain remarks, "From the point of view of the sanctification of the servants of God, it matters little whether a malady has one cause or another. The same virtues can be exercised in either case". The important point is that Hopkins did interpret his crucifixion in supernatural terms. And where is there a better exegesis of Hopkins' condition than in such passages (which could be multiplied indefinitely) as the following, in which God speaks to St. Catherine of Siena in her famous dialogue:

> In order to raise the soul from imperfection, I withdraw myself from her sentiment, depriving her of former consolations . . . which I do in order to humiliate her, and cause her to seek Me in truth, and to prove her in the light of faith, so that she come to prudence. Then, if she love Me without thought of self, and with lively faith and with hatred of her own sensuality, she rejoices in

---

* honeycombs (*cf.* "Delicious").

the time of trouble, deeming herself unworthy of peace and quiet-
ness of mind. Now comes the second of three things which I told
thee, that is to say: how the soul arrives at perfection, and what
she does when she is perfect. That is what she does. Though she
perceives that I have withdrawn Myself, she does not, on that
account, look back; but perseveres with humility in her exercises,
remaining barred in the house of self-knowledge, and, continuing
to dwell therein, awaits with lively faith the coming of the Holy
Spirit. . . . This is what the soul does in order to rise from imperfection and arrive at perfection, and it is to this end, namely,
that she may arrive at perfection, that I withdraw from her, not
by grace, but by sentiment. Once more do I leave her so that she
may see and know her defects, so that feeling herself deprived of
consolation and afflicted by pain, she may recognize her own
weakness, and learn how incapable she is of stability or persever-
ance, thus cutting down to the very root of spiritual self-love;
for this should be the end and purpose of all her self-knowledge,
to rise above herself, mounting the throne of conscience, and not
permitting the sentiment of imperfect love to turn again in its
death-struggle, but, with correction and reproof, digging up the
root of self-love with the knife of self-hatred and the love of
virtue.

It must be recalled that for Hopkins spiritual aridity was poetic
aridity. He wrote few poems after the sonnets of 1884-5. In 1886
only one poem, "On the Portrait of Two Beautiful Young People",
was added to his body of verse. The year after, "Tom's Garland"
and "Harry Ploughman" were written during a summer holiday
at Dromore (1887); these are only implicitly religious poems, for
Hopkins had attained that wholeness (so seldom possible since
the Reformation) in which certain premises can be taken for
granted. "Harry Ploughman" shows his delight in natural acts
perfectly performed, and it is a poetic counterpart of his prose
notes for an address on the Principle and Foundation, where he
wrote, "When a man is in God's grace and free from mortal sin,
then everything that he does, so long as there is no sin in it, gives
God glory and what does not give him glory has some, however
little, sin in it. It is not only prayer that gives God glory but
work".[4] "Tom's Garland", that difficult and cryptic sonnet, is an
admirable poetic statement of the Catholic view of the relation
of the individual to the state; implicit in it is the doctrine
of the Mystical Body. Then during the last two years of his
life. 1888-9, Hopkins composed five new poems. With the study

of this last group our survey of some forty religious poems comes to an end.

Hopkins' production was falling off; and two of the poems of this final group are devoted to his aridity. From his "winter-world" he addresses a severely chastened sonnet to Bridges. Entitled simply "To R.B.", he sends an explanation that in his state of desolation he lacks the initial joyous inspiration which he considers essential to the genesis of poetry. The octet is calm and controlled in its restrained expression; the sestet pulses with the more personal application to his own state:

> Sweet fire the sire of muse, my souls needs this,
> I want the one rapture of an inspiration.
> O then if in my lagging lines you miss
> The roll, the rise, the carol, the creation,
> My winter world, that scarcely breathes that bliss
> Now, yields you, with some sighs, our explanation.

E. E. Phare has remarked on the superb art of this last line, which "conveys, almost onomatopoetically, a strong sense of the difficulty which beset his muse in producing even a few scanty words. The sonnet goes into a diminuendo down to the last flat dull word 'explanation'."

"Some sighs" would be a weak epithet indeed to apply to the terrible anguish of desolation which he expresses in the second poem (No. 50) devoted to his aridity. Direct in its terrible question, he asks Christ the reason for his bitter impotence. His bleeding heart cries out in the midst of its affliction as it echoes Jeremias:

> Thou art indeed just, Lord, if I contend
> With thee; but, sir, so what I plead is just.

Then comes the agonizing question:

> Why do sinners' ways prosper? and why must
> Disappointment all I endeavour end?
> Wert thou my enemy, O thou my friend,
> How wouldst thou worse, I wonder, than thou dost
> Defeat, thwart me? Oh, the sots and thralls of lust
> Do in spare hours more thrive than I that spend,
> Sir, life upon thy cause.

And he contrasts his own interior desert with the fecundity around him:

See, banks and brakes*

Now, leavèd how thick! lacèd they are again
With fretty chervil,† look, and fresh wind shakes
Them; birds build—but not I build; no, but strain,
Time's eunuch, and not breed one work that wakes.

This is an echo from his letters and already carries with it the answer, "It is for the kingdom of heaven's sake", for perfection, for Christ. The final line is a prayer, a prayer for deliverance from the desert of his calvary:

Mine, O thou lord of life, send my roots rain.

"Never, I think", Aldous Huxley has written, "has the just man's complaint against the universe been put more forcibly, worded more tersely and fiercely than in Hopkins' sonnet. God's answer is found in that most moving, most magnificent and profoundest poem of antiquity, the Book of Job." Yes, but the ultimate answer, as the priest knew, really comes from the Cross.

Occasionally during these last years the poet must have felt that man's problems, however difficult, are actually poor and meagre; for one poem (No. 69) conveys this mood in its lines:

The shepherd's brow, fronting forked lightning, owns
The horror and the havoc and the glory
Of it. Angels fall, they are towers, from heaven—a story
Of just, majestical, and giant groans.
But man—we, scaffold of score brittle bones;
Who breathe, from groundlong babyhood to hoary
Age gasp; whose breath is our *memento mori*—
What bass is *our* viol for tragic tones?

But the answer to this gloomy minimizing is explicit in a sonnet, "In honour of St. Alphonsus Rodriguez". It might well have been written to celebrate Hopkins' own devotion to the ideals of St. Ignatius during his twenty-one years in the Society; for like St. Alphonsus' his was also "the war within". The poem first expresses the recognition that all give to the heroic deed which shines before their eyes:

Honour is flashed off exploit, so we say;
And those strokes once that gashed flesh or galled shield
Should tongue that time now, trumpet now that field
And, on the fighter, forge his glorious day.
On Christ they do and on the martyr may.

* Thickets.   † The aromatic herb.

But there is also an interior consecration and martyrdom hidden
from others:

> But be the war within, the brand we wield
> Unseen, the heroic breast not outward-steeled,
> Earth hears no hurtle then from fiercest fray.

But St. Alphonsus'—and Hopkins' own—fierce fray was heard by
Him who scans all things:

> Yet God (that hews mountain and continent,
> Earth, all, out; who, with trickling increment,
> Veins violets and tall trees makes more and more)
> Could crowd career with conquest while there went
> Those years and years by of world without event
> That in Majorca Alfonso watched the door.

"Strung by duty", the Jesuit had affirmed, "is strained to beauty",
but this is a beauty that can often be seen only from the high-
roads of the spiritual life, where "immortal beauty is death with
duty" (No. 59). The priest-poet here reaffirms with triumphant
vigour the realization which had found an earlier expression when
he was just about to be ordained as a priest:

> Shéer plód makes plough down sillion
> Shine, and blue-bleak embers, ah my dear,
> Fall, gall themselves, and gash gold-vermilion.

One poem remains to be considered, a wonderfully different
poem written during the last year of his life. "That Nature is a
Heraclitean Fire and of the Comfort of the Resurrection" is not
taut and chastened like most of the poems of 1885-9. Elaborately
patterned and variegated, it exploits the potentialities of the
language in its exuberant orchestration.

The opening lines recreate the panorama of the dappled world;
the rhythm suggests, perhaps, the kaleidoscopic parade of reality
in a never-ending march from fire to earth, earth to fire, from dust
to flesh, and flesh to dust. Indeed all the world is included in this
all-embracing Heraclitean flux: "Million-fuelèd, nature's bonfire
burns on". Even man is included in the holocaust. And in the
midst of this terrifying transiency, the poet cannot help crying out:

> O pity and indignation! Manshape, that shone
> Sheer off, disseveral, a star, ' death blots black out; nor mark
>   Is any of him at all so stark
> But vastness blurs and time ' beats level.

Then ring out the buoyant optimism and wildly triumphant realization that this life is a refining fire of purgation and that man will be snatched from the conflagration and emerge, all conflicts resolved, a new being:

> Enough! the Resurrection,
> A heart's-clarion! Away grief's gasping, ' joyless days, dejection.
> Across my foundering deck shone
> A beacon, an eternal beam. ' Flesh fade, and mortal trash
> Fall to the residuary worm; ' world's wildfire, leave but ash:

Then comes the final apocalypse; the outburst is similar to the vision of Christ in "The Wreck of the Deutschland"; for now the lines trumpet a man's own final "achieve of, the mastery of the thing":

> In a flash, at a trumpet crash,
> I am all at once what Christ is, ' since he was what I am, and
> This Jack, joke, poor potsherd, ' patch, matchwood, immortal diamond,
> Is immortal diamond.

Here is the hope and joy of the Fourth Week of the Spiritual Exercises. Here is the destiny of man, his divinization, in a human mode, in Christ. Here is the echo of Hopkins' deathbed words thrice repeated. "I am so happy, I am so happy, I am so happy".

Appendix

DUNS SCOTUS AND HOPKINS

HOPKINS, it has been stated in the text, was drawn to Duns Scotus because he found in him a justification for his own analysis of beauty; "both of them had the same experience of 'forms' as sharply individual and particular".

What is distinctive in Scotus' theory of the constitution of reality is best seen in contrast with St. Thomas. In general the Schoolmen conceived all created things as containing two principles, the principle of matter and the principle of form, both terms being here understood in the philosophical sense. These two exist as correlatives, and together make up the *compositum*. Neither exists without the other.

St. Thomas held that the form determines the species of a thing, while the matter determines its individuality within the species. For him the form determined the "whatness" of a being, while the matter determined the "thisness". Together they make up the individual thing. Thus the Thomistic "principium individuationis" is a spatially determinant matter, "materia signata". Now, as frequently interpreted (or, rather, misinterpreted), St. Thomas would seem to sacrifice individuality in favour of the specific.

Scotus, on the other hand, as Etienne Gilson points out, almost destroys the unity of the species in order to safeguard the particularity of the individual, for he places the principle of individuation within the form itself. He distinguishes two things within the form, the universal nature common to all individuals of the same species, and the "haecceitas" or "thisness", which he calls the "entitas singularis" and which constitutes the individuality of the form.

Such a philosophical exposition of the sharp singularity of inner form which necessarily expresses itself in unity with outward distinctiveness appealed to the artist who, in looking about him, saw beauty as "the splendour of form shining on the proportioned parts of matter" in a highly organized and patterned variety expressive of inner particularity.

In his poetry, Hopkins tried to capture and give a life of their own to, to inscape his experiences not only of the world of nature, the world of variegated and differentiated beauties, but also to his experiences of the world of men, each distinct and individual and proclaiming his own selfhood.

We have seen Hopkins utilizing other aspects of the thought of Duns Scotus. The poet's emphasis on the operation of the will had Scotist leanings, though much the same accent may be found in the Spiritual Exercises and in the entire Jesuit tradition; so, too, Scotus may have helped to mould the sacramentalism expressed in his poems, though it is found in the Spiritual Exercises and in all of the scholastics, in one form or another. Several times he cites Scotus' passionate defence of the Immaculate Conception.

But in general we must remember that there is little that is daringly different from the general tradition of scholastic thought in anything that Hopkins wrote. Scotus himself was but a current in the large stream of the scholastic tradition, which was very flexible within its limits. Scotus, for instance, was not the only one to present a theory of individuation that differed from that of St. Thomas; Suarez, the great Jesuit theologian, held a theory of individuation closer to Scotus than to St. Thomas. The same is true of Suarez's theory of knowledge. Suarez further agreed with Scotus that even if Adam had not sinned, the Word would have become Incarnate.

While the professors of the Society of Jesus had advised its members to follow St. Thomas generally, they left considerable freedom for departing from his teaching. Some measure of the speculative freedom of the Jesuits may be gathered from what Newman wrote of them:

> It is plain that the body is not over-zealous about its theological traditions, or it certainly would not suffer Suarez to controvert with Molina, Viva with Vasquez, Passaglia with Petavius, and Faure with Suarez, Lugo and Valentia. In this intellectual freedom its members justly glory.

There is no reason, then, why Hopkins' admiration for Scotus should have brought him into any trouble with his fellow-Jesuits. But he was singular in his following of Scotus and sometimes he found a defence of his enthusiasms necessary; for he was in the midst of minds—among his Jesuit superiors and teachers as well as among his fellow scholastics—eager in the pursuit of truth. And Hopkins could not always convince others of what he himself thought. Father Lahey refers to these as "minor duels of intellect", and adds that he left St. Beuno's "with the reputation of being one of the best moral theologians among his contemporaries".

Hopkins went to Scotus, too, for an artist's epistemology. An experience of "inscape" requires such an epistemology. Rational knowledge, the *animus* of Claudel, is general, concerning itself with universals; it is abstract, concerning itself with forms abstracted from their concrete embodiment; it is conceptual.

But an experience of "inscape", Claudel's *anima*, would have to be a knowledge of a thing in its entirety; it would have to be individual, not general; concrete, not abstract; real, not conceptual. For aesthetic experience is concerned with the individuated "inner form" expressing itself in "outer form". It differs from rational knowledge inasmuch as the "inner form" is not abstracted from its sensible manifestation, but it is an experience of that "inner form" expressed in its sensible manifestation. The brilliance of form is enjoyed in the sensible.

Such an artist's theory of knowledge may more easily be found in the tomes of Duns Scotus than in Thomistic epistemology as it is usually outlined. (St. Thomas wrote no separate treatise on aesthetics and not until such studies as Maritain's *Art and Scholasticism* and Father Gilby's *Poetic Experience* have philosophers drawn up a satisfactory epistemology of aesthetic intuition out of scattered hints of St. Thomas.)

Both St. Thomas and Duns Scotus maintained that all knowledge has its origin in the senses. A famous maxim of the schoolmen was "particulare sentitur; universale intelligitur". But Scotus, unlike St. Thomas, contended that intellectual knowledge starts directly with the particular concrete thing and not with the universal, because for Scotus the particular is "part of" the form. According to his theory the intellect may know both the particular and the universal; the individual in its particular aspects is known by the "species specialissima", while its quiddity or whatness is known by the "species intelligibilis". For St. Thomas intellectual knowledge is of the universal: the intellect knows the "species intelligibilis"; only "per quandam reflexionem" can the intellect know the individual concrete thing.

Scotus, then, would seem to offer a theory of knowledge in which sense and intellect collaborate in one obviously simultaneous act to experience both the "species intelligibilis" (the particularized nature or form within) and the "species specialissima" (the outward sensible manifestation of inner form).

Such a theory of knowledge is eminently suited to the experience of beauty as "inscape", for it does not abstract the form from its concrete embodiment; rather, by one act of mind and senses it apprehends the inner in the outer, the splendour of individuated form shining upon proportioned parts of matter.

Scotus, as has been remarked, was not alone in emphasizing the ability of the mind to come directly in contact with the individual; Suarez defended an epistemology more akin to Scotus than to St. Thomas in this respect. Possibly it was because Newman's *Grammar of Assent* maintained the primacy of real over notional knowledge that Hopkins was so interested in the book and wanted to edit it with a commentary.

References

The following abbreviations have been used:

Letters to Bridges for *The Letters of Gerard Manley Hopkins to Robert Bridges* (ed. Claude Colleer Abbott), London: Oxford University Press, 1935.

Correspondence with Dixon for *The Correspondence of Gerard Manley Hopkins and Richard Watson Dixon* (ed. Claude Colleer Abbott), London: Oxford University Press, 1935.

Further Letters for *Further Letters of Gerard Manley Hopkins including his Correspondence with Coventry Patmore* (ed. Claude Colleer Abbott), London: Oxford University Press, 1938.

Note-books and Papers for *Note-books and Papers of Gerard Manley Hopkins* (ed. Humphry House), London: Oxford University Press, 1937.

Life for G. F. Lahey, S.J., *Gerard Manley Hopkins*, London: Oxford University Press, 1930.

All unpublished manuscripts to which reference is made are at Campion Hall, Oxford.

CHAPTER 1

1 *Further Letters*, pp. 237–8.
2 Quoted in *Life*, pp. 127–8.
3 *Further Letters*, p. 25.
4 *Letters to Bridges*, p. 48.
5 Quoted in *Life*, p. 19.
6 *Further Letters*, p. 254.
7 *Letters to Bridges*, p. 20.
8 Quoted in *Life*, p. 22.
9 *Note-books and Papers*, pp. 16–17.
10 *Ibid*, p. 21.
11 *Further Letters*, p. 11.
12 *Note-books and Papers*, p. 27.
13 Unpublished *ms*.
14 Quoted in *Life*, pp. 21–22.
15 *Further Letters*, p. 17.
16 *Ibid*.
17 *Ibid.*, p. 11.
18 *Letters to Bridges*, pp. 5–6.
19 *Further Letters*, p. 19.

20 *Ibid.*, pp. 255–6.
21 *Ibid.*, p. 20.
22 *Letters to Bridges*, p. 22.
23 *Further Letters*, p. 261.
24 *Ibid.*, p. 21.
25 *Note-books and Papers*, p. 53.

CHAPTER 2

1 *Note-books and Papers*, pp. 182 and 21.
2 *Ibid.*, p. 210.
3 *Ibid.*, p. 135 and p. 205.
4 *Ibid.*, p. 173.
5 *Ibid.*, p. 140.
6 *Correspondence with Dixon*, p. 135.
7 *Further Letters*, p. 225.
8 *Letters to Bridges*, p. 66.
9 *Note-books and Papers*, pp. 277 and 349.
10 *Further Letters*, p. 158.
11 *Note-books and Papers*, p. 161.
12 *Ibid.*, p. 198.
13 *Letters to Bridges*, p. 31.
14 *Note-books and Papers*, pp. 133–4.
15 *Correspondence with Dixon*, p. 141.
16 *Letters to Bridges*, p. 133.

CHAPTER 3

1 *Correspondence with Dixon*, p. 14.
2 *Note-books and Papers*, p. 337.
3 *Letters to Bridges*, p. 47.
4 *Note-books and Papers*, p. 332.
5 *Further Letters*, p. 9.
6 Unpublished *ms.*
7 *Ibid.*
8 *Ibid.*
9 *Ibid.*

CHAPTER 4

1 *Letters to Bridges*, p. 56.
2 *Note-books and Papers*, pp. 302–4.
3 *Ibid.*, p. 342.
4 *Ibid.*, p. 316.
5 *Correspondence with Dixon*, p. 20.
6 *Letters to Bridges*, p. 227.
7 *Ibid.*, p. 78.

8 Gerald Vann, *On Being Human*, New York: Sheed and Ward,1934, p. 57.
9 *Letters to Bridges*, p. 85.

CHAPTER 5

1 *Letters to Bridges*, p. 55.
2 *Correspondence with Dixon*, pp. 107 and 42.
3 *Letters to Bridges*, p. 136.
4 *Further Letters*, p. 146.
5 *Letters to Bridges*, p. 143.
6 *Correspondence with Dixon*, p. 97.
7 *Letters to Bridges*, p. 110.
8 *Further Letters*, p. 79.
9 *Ibid.*, pp. 78–80.
10 *Letters to Bridges*, p. 90.
11 *Correspondence with Dixon*, p. 29.
12 *Note-books and Papers*, p. xxxi.
13 *Letters to Bridges*, p. 57.
14 *Note-books and Papers*, p. 430
15 *Ibid.*, p. 431.
16 *Ibid.*, p. 432.
17 *Ibid.*, p. 286.
18 *Ibid.*, p. 433.
19 *Ibid.*
20 *Ibid.*, p. 287.
21 *Ibid.*
22 *Ibid.*, pp. 265–6.
23 *Ibid.*, p. 264.
24 *Ibid.*, p. 277.
25 *Ibid.*, pp. 280–1.
26 *Ibid.*, p. 267.
27 *Ibid.*, p. 268.
28 *Ibid.*, p. 269.
29 *Ibid.*, p. 261.
30 *Ibid.*, p. 263.
31 *Ibid.*, p. 264.
32 *Letters to Bridges*, pp. 187-8.
33 *Note-books and Papers*, p. 260.
34 *Letters to Bridges*, p. 279.

CHAPTER 6

1 Quoted in *Life*, p. 145.
2 *Ibid.*, p. 132.
3 *Letters to Bridges*, p. 95.

4 *Note-books and Papers*, p. 347.
5 Blanche Mary Kelly, *The Sudden Rose*, New York: Sheed and Ward, 1939, p. 159.
6 *Correspondence with Dixon*, p. 149.
7 *Note-books and Papers*, p. 288.
8 *Correspondence with Dixon*, p. 70.
9 *Ibid.*, p. 75.
10 *Ibid.*, pp. 75-6.
11 *Ibid.*, p. 89.
12 *Ibid.*, p. 88.
13 *Ibid.*, p. 102.
14 Unpublished *ms.*
15 *Note-books and Papers*, p. 332.
16 *Ibid.*, p. 321.
17 *Ibid.*, p. 342.
18 *Ibid.*, pp. 302-3.
19 Unpublished *ms.*
20 *Note-books and Papers*, pp. 309-10.
21 *Ibid.*, p. 332.
22 *Ibid.*, p. 343.
23 *Ibid.*, p. 336.

CHAPTER 7

1 Quoted in *Life*, pp. 143-4.
2 *Ibid.*, p. 142.
3 *Ibid.*, p. 141.
4 *Letters to Bridges*, p. 190.
5 *Ibid.*, p. 198
6 *Ibid.*, p. 229; *Correspondence with Dixon*, p. 151; *Ibid.*, p. 136.
7 *Letters to Bridges*, p. 236.
8 *Ibid.*, p. 296.
9 *Note-books and Papers*, pp. 181-2.
10 *Further Letters*, p. 84.
11 *Letters to Bridges*, p. 47.
12 *Ibid.*, p. 104.
13 *Ibid.*, pp. 214-5.
14 *Further Letters*, pp. 109-10.
15 Quoted in *Life*, p. 145.
16 Rev. Martin C. D'Arcy, "Gerard Manley Hopkins", *Great Catholics* (ed. Claude Williamson), New York: Macmillan, pp. 359-60.
17 *Letters to Bridges*, p. 222.
18 *Ibid.*, pp. 284-5.
19 *Ibid.*, pp. 262, 271, 290.
20 *Ibid.*, p. 251.

21 Quoted in *Life*, p. 142.
22 *Further Letters*, pp. 265-6.
23 *Ibid.*, pp. 218-20.
24 *Letters to Bridges*, p. 231.
25 *Further Letters*, p. 85.
26 *Letters to Bridges*, p. 24.
27 *Correspondence with Dixon*, pp. 14-15.
28 *Ibid.*, p. 15.
29 *Ibid.*, p. 28.
30 *Letters to Bridges*, p. 66.
31 *Correspondence with Dixon*, p. 6.
32 *Ibid.*
33 *Ibid.*, p. 15.
34 *Letters to Bridges*, p. 197.
35 *Ibid.*, p. 61.
36 *Note-books and Papers*, pp. 304-5.
37 *Correspondence with Dixon*, p. 33.
38 *Ibid.*, pp. 88-9.
39 *Ibid.*, p. 90.
40 *Ibid.*, p. 93.
41 *Ibid.*, p. 90.
42 *Ibid.*, pp. 93-4.
43 *Ibid.*, p. 94.
44 *Ibid.*, p. 96.
45 *Ibid.*, p. 94.
46 *Letters to Bridges*, p. 270.
47 *Ibid.*, p. 231.
48 *Ibid.*, pp. 218-9.
49 *Ibid.*, pp. 221-2.
50 *Ibid.*, p. 270.
51 Unpublished *ms.*
52 *Correspondence with Dixon*, p. 8.
53 *Letters to Bridges*, p. 221.
54 *Ibid.*, p. 196.
55 *Correspondence with Dixon*, p. 8.
56 *Letters to Bridges*, p. 60.
57 Quoted in *Life*, p. 53.
58 *Further Letters*, p. xxiv.
59 *Letters to Bridges*, p. 187.
60 *Ibid.*, p. 66.
61 *Ibid.*, p. 270.
62 *Further Letters*, p. 109.
63 Quoted in *Life*, p. 66.
64 *Letters to Bridges*, p. 25.

65 *Note-books and Papers*, p. 417.
66 *Correspondence with Dixon*, pp. 137–8.
67 *Note-books and Papers*, pp. 416–7.

CHAPTER 8

1 *Correspondence with Dixon*, p. 150.
2 *Note-books and Papers*, pp. 339 and 416.
3 *Letters to Bridges*, p. 221.
4 *Note-books and Papers*, p. 304.

Index

Abbott, C. C., 58, 124, 126
Addis, W. E., 14, 18
Aestheticism, 4–9, 12, 15, 34
"Alphonsus Rodriguez, St", 153
alter Christus, 28, 41, 49, 71, 81, 101, 105
Aquinas, St. Thomas, 17, 35, 39, 54, 61, 69, 84, 105, 156–9
Aristotle, 34
Aridity, 124, 128–9, 132, 135, 141–52
Arnold, Matthew, 7, 11
Asceticism, 4, 9, 15, 25, 28, 37–8, 51, 55, 69, 117–8, 128–9
"Ash-Boughs", 55
Augustine, St., 42, 59–60

Baillie, Alexander W. M., 30, 74, 110–11, 115
Balliol, 4, 7, 11, 14, 21
Beauty, ix, 2–11, 15, 16, 23, 31–9, 52–64, 68, 71, 90–5, 138–41, 154
Bedford Leigh, 73–5, 108, 119
Bernard, St., 104
Blessed Virgin, The, 57–8, 83, 103–4
"Blessed Virgin (The) compared . . .' 103–4
Bonaventure, St., 54
Bridges, Robert, 1, 8, 14, 55, 102, 112, 125–7, 141, 145–8
— letters to, 8, 20–2, 30, 33–4, 38, 41–2, 47, 58, 65–7, 73–7, 84–91, 94–5, 108–12, 115–16, 118, 123, 129–31, 136, 143
— sonnet to, 152
"Brothers, The", 87, 90
"Bugler's First Communion, The", 88–9

"Caged Skylark, The", 69–70
"Candle Indoors, The", 97
"Carrion Comfort", 147–8
Catherine of Siena, St., 150
Chesterfield, 25, 73, 110
Chesterton, G. K., 56
Claudel, Paul, 158
Cobbett, 74
Conversion, 5, 17–19

Cross, The, ix, 41–2, 45–6, 48, 69, 71–2, 81, 83, 85, 100, 124, 127, 136–7, 147, 153

D'Arcy, Fr. M.C., vii, ix, x, 111–12
De Grandmaison, Père, 130
De Ravignan, Fr., 26
Desolation. *See* Aridity
Dixon, Canon R. W., 30, 38, 40, 64, 73–5, 86, 98–9, 109, 115–27, 136, 140
Dolben, Digby, 14
Dublin, 25, 99, 102, 106–16, 122–3, 128–9, 132, 136, 141–4
Dublin Note-Book, 136–7, 141
"Duns Scotus's Oxford", 64–5

Eckhart, 37
Eliot, T. S., 7, 8, 127
Essays and Reviews, 11, 13

Fall of man, the, 69, 81–3, 91–2, 96
Farm Street Church, 73, 80
"Felix Randall", 88–9
Fletcher, J. G., 128
Francis of Assisi, St, 47, 53, 56

Gardner, W. W. H., 36
Geldart, E. M., 14
Gilby, Fr., 158
Gilson, Etienne, 156
"God's Grandeur", 62–4, 76, 102
Graves, Robert, 59, 148

"Habit of Perfection, The", 16
"Handsome Heart, The", 90–1
"Harry Ploughman", 151
"Heaven-Haven" ("Rest"), 17
Henderson, Philip, 55
"Henry Purcell", 88, 144
"Heraclitean Fire", x, 86, 154
High Church party. *See* Tractarianism
Highgate poems, 1–3, 9, 17, 32, 127–8
"Hope holds to Christ . . .", 136–7
Hopkins, Manley, 20
Hügel, Von, 139–40
"Hurrahing in Harvest", 58
Huxley, Aldous, 153

"I wake and feel the fell of dark", 145

Ignatius, St., and the Society of Jesus, 22–6, 29, 32, 36, 99, 118–19, 122, 149, 153

Constitutions, 25, 55, 97

Contemplation to gain Love, 29, 37–8, 59, 63

Directory, 26–8, 59, 133

Hopkins' Commentary on the Exercises, 25, 42–3, 49, 63, 66, 92, 100–4, 122, 141

Institute, 98

Principle and Foundation, 27, 28, 37, 52, 60, 66, 81, 117, 151

Rules, 55, 97, 144

Spiritual Exercises, 24–32, 36–7, 41–4, 51–2, 59–60, 69, 81–2, 86, 96–7, 111, 117–18, 124, 127, 132–6, 144–5, 149, 155–7

The Two Standards, 42, 142

Imitation of Christ, The, 26, 96, 132–3, 135, 137, 147–9

Immaculate Conception, The, 83, 157

"In the Valley of the Elwy", 66–8, 102

Incarnation, the, 44–5, 49, 51, 70, 83–5, 103

"Inscape", 32–6, 53–4, 58, 139, 156, 158–9

"Instress," 31–2, 44, 58, 66

Jesus, Society of. *See* Ignatius, Saint

John of the Cross, St., 129–33, 145

Journal, 30–37, 57, 66, 109

Jowett, 10, 11, 12, 106

Keats, 2–4, 6, 8, 9, 51

Kelly, Bernard, 41, 49

"Kingfishers catch fire, As", 104

Knox, Mgr Ronald, 55

Lacordaire, 17

La Farge, Fr., 25

Lahey, Fr. G. F., 21, 157

"Lantern out of Doors, The", 68

Lataste, Marie, 124, 132–4, 147

"Leaden Echo and the Golden Echo, The", 93–5, 124, 139

Leavis, F. R., 142–3

Lewis, David, 34

"Liberalism", 10, 11, 13, 17

Liddon, H. P., 12–15, 21

Liverpool, 73–5, 77, 79, 108, 110, 119

"Loss of the Eurydice", 67, 85, 125

Lucas, Herbert, 34

Machen, Arthur, 128

Manresa House, Roehampton, 23–5, 40, 73, 115

Maritain, Jacques, 33, 39, 51, 54, 158

"May Magnificat", 57, 103

"Morning, Mid-day, and Evening Sacrifice", 95

Morris, Brande, 34

Morris, William 6, 7

"My own heart let me have more pity on" (No. 47), 148

Mysticism, ix, 51, 129–31

Newman, John Henry, 4, 10–14, 18–24, 106–7, 113–14, 159

"No worst, there is none . . .", 129, 146

"Nondum", 18, 50

Novitiate, 1, 3, 7, 22–6. 35, 37, 40, 98, 109, 115–16

"On a piece of Music", 38–9

Oratory School, 22, 110

Oxford, 4–18

Hopkins's poems and papers at, 1, 9, 15–19, 23, 30, 32, 50, 120, 128

St. Aloysius', 8; 64, 73, 75

Paraclete, the, 77, 79

Parish work, 25, 73–5, 86, 119

Passion, the, 29, 41–2, 45, 48, 84, 147

Pater, Walter, 7–11, 17, 55

"Patience, hard thing . . .", 149

Patmore, Coventry, 3, 30, 44, 112, 114, 125–7, 131

Pattison, Mark, 11–12

Paul, St., 42, 54

"Peace", 96, 99

Phare, E. E., 152

Phillipson, Dom Wulstan, 107

"Pied Beauty", 53–6, 102

Plato, 38, 54, 69

Plotinus, 92

Politics, 112–14

Pollen, Fr. J., 25

"Portrait of Two Beautiful Young People, on the", 90, 138, 140–1, 151

Poulain, Père, 130, 150, 154

Pre-raphaelitism, 6, 7

Purcell, Henry, 88, 138, 144
Purgative Way, the, 37, 71
Puritanism, 51, 55–6
Pusey, E. B., 10–14, 21

Rationalism, 5, 10–15
Raynal, Fr., 18, 22
Read, Herbert, 55
Redemption, 41–9, 83, 89, 100–1
"Rest", 17
Resurrection, the, 70, 86, 154–5
"Ribblesdale", 102
Richards, I. A., 70
Riding, Laura, 59, 148
Ritualism, 8, 14, 15
Rodriguez, St. Alphonsus, 153
"Rosa Mystica", 103
Rossetti, D. G., 6
Ruskin, 6, 7, 11

Sacramentalism, 35–8, 51–4, 58, 61–3, 68, 87–9, 102
Sacrifice, 100, 120–4, 136, 154
St. Beuno's, 25, 30, 34, 66, 93, 158
"St. Winefred's Well", 93, 122
Scotus, Duns, 32–7, 51–4, 64, 83–4, 156–9
"Sea and the Skylark, The", 65, 76, 102
Sermons, 33, 45, 73, 76–86, 91, 96, 104
"Shepherd's brow (The) . . .", 153
"Soldier, The", 86
"Spelt from Sibyl's Leaves", 138, 141–3
"Spring", 68, 90

"Spring and Fall", 92
"Starlight Night, The", 56–7, 102
Stonyhurst, 25, 34, 58, 101–4, 107, 126
Suso, Blessed Henry, 136

Tertianship, 24, 87, 97–101, 104, 119, 122–4
"Thou art indeed just, Lord...", 152–3
"To his watch," 93
"To seem the stranger . . .", 114, 144–5
"To what serves mortal Beauty?", 138–40
"Tom's Garland", 151
Tractarianism, 5, 9–15, 20
Trinity, the, 63, 84

Unitive Way, the, 28–9, 37, 129–31
Urquhart, Rev. E. W., 19

Vann, Fr. G., 37
"Vision of the Mermaids", 2, 9, 53
"Voice from the World, A", 15

Wales, 25, 31–2, 66, 68, 74, 93
Watkin, E. I., 34
Welsh language, 31–2
Whitman, 55
"Windhover, The", 55, 70–1, 125
Winwar, Frances, 55
"Wreck of the Deutschland, The", 30, 40–52, 59, 67, 80, 82–3, 103, 113, 116, 120, 125, 136–7, 147, 155

Zabel, Morton, 142